INTERLAKEN
Travel Guide 2025-2026

Explore adventure, culture, local hidden gems, and unique outdoor experiences in the Swiss Alps

WALTER L. WILKERSON

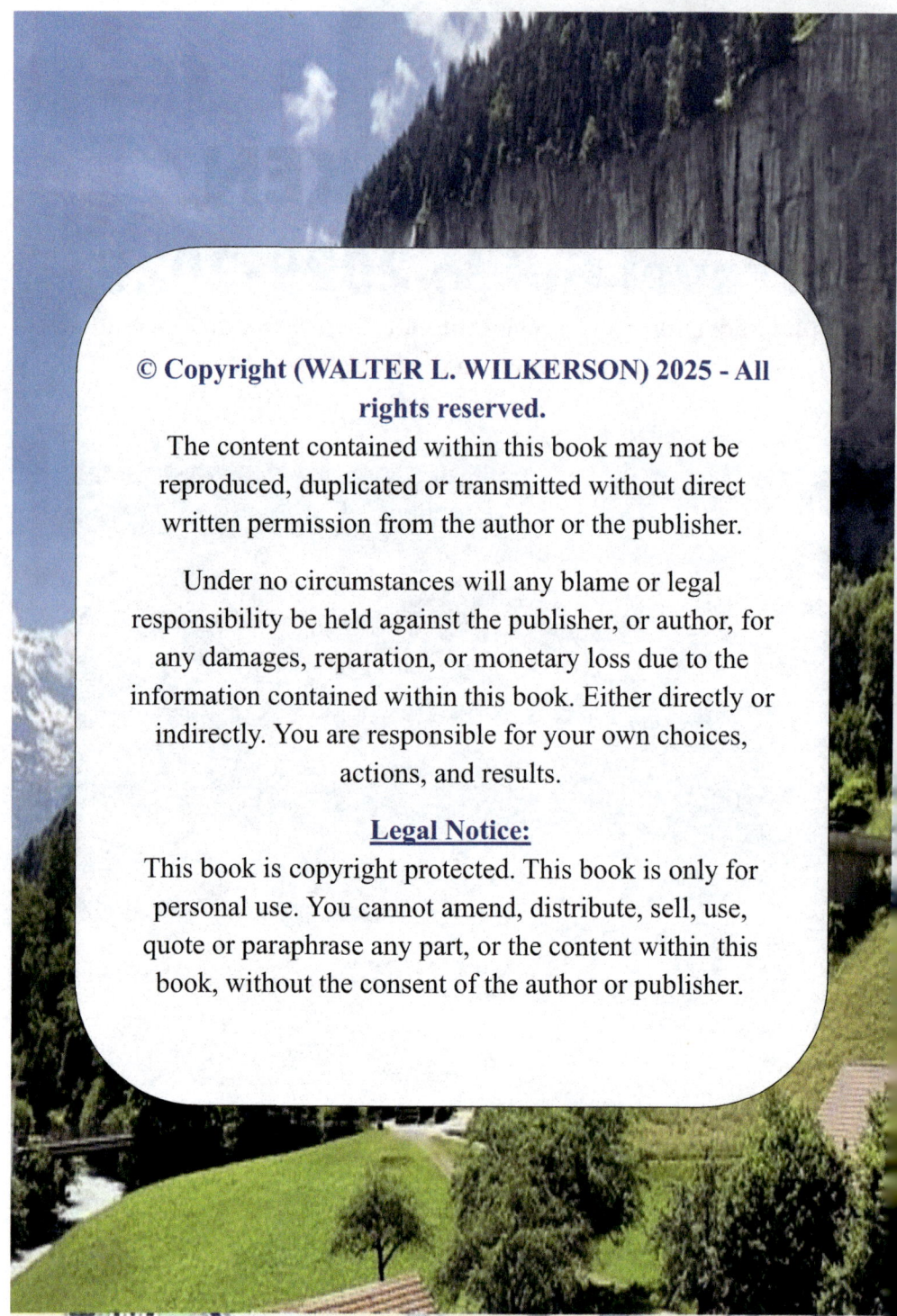

© Copyright (WALTER L. WILKERSON) 2025 - All rights reserved.

The content contained within this book may not be reproduced, duplicated or transmitted without direct written permission from the author or the publisher.

Under no circumstances will any blame or legal responsibility be held against the publisher, or author, for any damages, reparation, or monetary loss due to the information contained within this book. Either directly or indirectly. You are responsible for your own choices, actions, and results.

Legal Notice:

This book is copyright protected. This book is only for personal use. You cannot amend, distribute, sell, use, quote or paraphrase any part, or the content within this book, without the consent of the author or publisher.

Dedication

To those captivated by the enchanting spirit of Interlaken, where snow-capped peaks rise above crystal-blue lakes and alpine air carries whispers of adventure. It is not only the breathtaking views from Harder Kulm (46°41'2.6"N 7°51'23.4"E) or the serene charm of Lake Brienz (46°43'1.2"N 7°57'37.9"E) that inspire, but also the gentle rhythm of cowbells drifting across mountain pastures, the scent of pine carried on the breeze, and the soft hush of waves along Lake Thun's shores near Neuhaus (46°40'43.1"N 7°45'59.3"E).

To those who wander the vibrant streets of Höheweg (46°41'1.5"N 7°51'9.1"E), glide across the turquoise waters at Iseltwald (46°43'43.5"N 7°58'21.8"E), or marvel at the cascading beauty of Giessbach Falls (46°44'28.1"N 8°1'38.9"E)—this guide is for you. To the hikers scaling the rugged trails of Schynige Platte (46°39'50.8"N 7°49'24.3"E), the dreamers chasing sunsets at Harder Ridge, the thrill-seekers soaring above the valley on paraglides, and the curious souls seeking culture in quaint alpine villages—Interlaken promises something unforgettable at every turn.

And to Interlaken—a destination where nature, tradition, and adventure converge, where the grandeur of the Bernese Alps meets the timeless calm of glacier-fed lakes. May your journey here awaken your senses, enrich your spirit, and leave you with memories as lasting as the mountains themselves.

About The Author

Walter L. Wilkerson brings you the *Interlaken Travel Guide 2025–2026*, offering an expert's perspective on one of Europe's most breathtaking alpine destinations. With years of experience exploring Interlaken's pristine lakes, towering peaks, and charming villages, Walter provides invaluable insights for both first-time visitors and seasoned adventurers.

This guide dives deep into the heart of the Jungfrau Region, from the lively promenade of Höheweg (46°41'1.5"N 7°51'9.1"E) to the panoramic views atop Harder Kulm (46°41'2.6"N 7°51'23.4"E), highlighting must-see attractions as well as hidden gems often overlooked by tourists. Drawing on his extensive knowledge of Interlaken's culture, outdoor activities, and culinary scene, Walter invites readers to experience the region's seamless blend of natural beauty, traditional charm, and modern adventure.

Whether you're cruising the emerald waters of Lake Brienz (46°43'1.2"N 7°57'37.9"E), hiking the scenic trails of Schynige Platte (46°39'50.8"N 7°49'24.3"E), or paragliding above the Lauterbrunnen Valley (46°35'31.0"N 7°54'33.7"E), Walter's guide ensures your Interlaken journey will be immersive, enriching, and unforgettable. With every page, Interlaken transforms from a destination into an experience—a place where alpine wonders, cultural encounters, and adventure converge to create lasting memories.

About The Book

Interlaken Travel Guide 2025–2026 by Walter L. Wilkerson is your ultimate companion to Interlaken—a destination where alpine beauty, crystal-clear lakes, and adventurous spirit converge. From the towering Jungfrau peaks to serene lakeshores and charming Swiss villages, Interlaken offers an unforgettable experience for every traveler. Whether you're hiking the trails of Schynige Platte (46°39'50.8"N 7°49'24.3"E), cruising the turquoise waters of Lake Brienz (46°43'1.2"N 7°57'37.9"E), or exploring the vibrant streets of Höheweg (46°41'1.5"N 7°51'9.1"E), this guide helps you immerse yourself fully in the region's unique offerings.

Perfect for both first-time visitors and seasoned explorers, this guide offers practical advice, curated itineraries, and insider tips to help you make the most of your journey. Discover must-see landmarks, secret viewpoints, traditional eateries, and strategies for navigating the Jungfrau Region seamlessly. Whether enjoying panoramic views from Harder Kulm (46°41'2.6"N 7°51'23.4"E) or visiting the Alpine Garden at Schynige Platte (46°39'58.7"N 7°49'12.8"E), you'll feel deeply connected to Interlaken's landscapes and culture.

With sections on accommodation, transportation, and seasonal planning, this guide ensures every detail of your trip is covered. Explore charming villages like Lauterbrunnen (46°35'31.0"N 7°54'33.7"E) and Grindelwald (46°37'29.5"N 8°2'21.3"E), sample authentic Swiss delicacies, and discover where tradition meets modern adventure.

With GPS coordinates, historical insights, and eco-friendly travel tips, this guide helps you engage with Interlaken on a deeper level. Whether you're paragliding, hiking the Eiger Trail (46°34'33.1"N 8°0'47.8"E), or relaxing by Lake Thun (46°43'49.1"N 7°37'44.5"E), the *Interlaken Travel Guide 2025–2026* provides everything you need for an unforgettable adventure.

Table of Contents

PROLOGUE 6

Introduction to Interlaken 10

Chapter 1: Essential Travel Information 14

Chapter 2: Transportation & Getting Around Interlaken 18

Chapter 3: Where to Stay in Interlaken 22

Chapter 4: Top Attractions in and around Interlaken 26

Chapter 5: Local Cuisine in interlaken 36

Chapter 6: Activities and Experiences 40

Chapter 7: Itineraries for Different Types of Travelers 46

Chapter 8: What to Do and What Not to Do in the Alps 50

Chapter 9: Shopping in Interlaken 54

Chapter 10: Responsible and Sustainable Travel 58

Chapter 11: Nature and Wildlife in Interlaken 62

Chapter 12: Local Art and Cultural Experiences 66

Chapter 13: Hidden Beaches and Secret Spots 70

Chapter 14: Tips for Traveling with Kids 74

Chapter 15: Interlaken's Nightlife and After-Hours Scene 78

Chapter 16: Best Luxury Experiences in Interlaken 82

Chapter 17: Social Media Spots and Instagram-Worthy Locations . 86

Chapter 18: Local Language and Phrases Guide 90

Chapter 19: Quick Reference & Resources 96

Maps 104

Bonus Section 105

PROLOGUE

I first came to Interlaken more than a decade ago, expecting it to be just another alpine stopover on my route across Switzerland. Instead, it became the place I return to most often, my anchor in the Bernese Oberland. From here, I've reached valleys shaped by waterfalls, lakes edged with quiet villages, and high summits where the air is thin and the views feel limitless. Each visit has taught me something new—where to walk at sunrise, how to avoid queues, which trails reveal silence. Interlaken is not just a destination—it is the launch point of countless alpine journeys.

Why This Guide Was Written

I wrote this guide because Interlaken is easy to admire but harder to navigate without planning. Many travelers come for a day or two, take the obvious tours, and leave without seeing the depth that locals know. My goal is to provide you with practical tools to travel smarter: how to utilize passes, when to time lifts, and where to find views without crowds. This is not about chasing postcards; it is about balance. I want you to move confidently, waste less time in queues, and enjoy both the celebrated highlights and the quiet corners that are often overlooked.

How to Use This Book

Think of this book as a tool you carry, not just something you read. Each chapter is arranged step by step, with details you can apply the moment you arrive. Exact addresses and GPS coordinates are provided, allowing you to add them to your maps without any guesswork. Lists such as "Quick-Start Highlights" give you options when time is short. The "Bucket List" section helps you cover essentials before leaving. I encourage you to read broadly, but use each section as a reference in real time—whether you're standing in Interlaken Ost station or looking for a quiet lakeside path.

About the Author and Research Process

My advice is based on experience, not theory. I have visited Interlaken multiple times, in various seasons and under different weather conditions. I've tested transport passes like the Jungfrau Travel Pass, joined group tours, and also moved alone at my own pace. I stayed in hostels, hotels, and lakeside chalets to compare value. I walked the transfer routes between stations and piers, timing each one. I ate in tourist cafés and tucked-away bakeries to see the difference. Every recommendation has been cross-checked against schedules, maps, and field notes to ensure accuracy. What you find in these pages are the exact methods I used myself. Quick-Start Highlights

If you have one day, these save time:

- Ride the Harder Kulm Funicular, Harderstrasse 34, 3800 Interlaken, Switzerland [46.68953, 7.85721] – 10 minutes to the top.
- Walk the Neuhaus Strandbad lakeshore, Seestrasse 121, 3800 Unterseen, Switzerland [46.67786, 7.81691].
- Take a Lake Brienz cruise from Interlaken Ost pier, Untere Bönigstrasse 5, 3800 Interlaken [46.69042, 7.86903].
- End with dinner on the terrace of Victoria-Jungfrau Grand Hotel, Höheweg 41, 3800 Interlaken [46.68635, 7.85774].

Top 10 Experiences in Interlaken

1. Stand on the **Two Lakes Bridge** at Harder Kulm.
2. Ride the **Eiger Express gondola** to Eigergletscher.
3. Board a boat to **Giessbach Falls** and ride its historic funicular.
4. Hike the **Schynige Platte Panorama Trail**.
5. Explore **St. Beatus Caves**, Staatsstrasse 30, 3800 Sundlauenen [46.68431, 7.78172].
6. Walk under **Staubbach Falls** in Lauterbrunnen.
7. Stroll Interlaken's **Höheweg promenade** at sunset.
8. Watch paragliders land on **Höhematte Park**, Höheweg, 3800 Interlaken [46.68591, 7.85981].
9. Take the **Brienz Rothorn steam train**.

10. Visit **Ballenberg Open-Air Museum** in Brienz.

Editor's Picks: Best of Interlaken

- Best quick view: **Harder Kulm terrace**
- Best rainy-day option: **St. Beatus Caves**
- Best family walk: **Lake Brienz east shore**
- Best sunrise: **Neuhaus lakeshore**
- Best splurge meal: **Victoria-Jungfrau terrace**

Interlaken Bucket List: 10 Things to Do Before You Leave

- Ride the first Harderbahn of the morning.
- Swim or wade at Neuhaus.
- Picnic in Höhematte Park.
- Taste Meiringen meringues in their hometown.
- Walk the Lauterbrunnen Valley floor.
- Take a Lake Thun cruise to Spiez.
- Photograph Giessbach Falls from the bridge.
- Order rösti in a mountain hut.
- Visit the Alpine Garden at Schynige Platte.
- End one day watching paragliders land at dusk.

Only Locals Know: Insider Tips and Hidden Rituals

- Take the Harderbahn in the last hour before sunset—queues drop.
- Sit on the right side of the Lake Brienz boats as they depart for better photos.
- Start the Beatenbucht funicular to Niederhorn early for quiet cabins.

- Buy snacks at Coop Restaurant Interlaken Ost, Untere Bönigstrasse 10, 3800 Interlaken [46.68988, 7.86943] before boarding boats.
- Carry small cash for lockers and bakeries.

How to Scan the QR Code for Interlaken Directions

Using the QR codes on the Interlaken Hotels and Museums maps is the fastest way to access Google Maps and get directions directly to your desired destination. Follow these simple steps:

Step 1: Open Your Smartphone's Camera or QR Scanner
- Scan QR codes using your smartphone's camera app.
- Download a free QR code scanner if scanning is unsupported.

Step 2: Point the Camera at the QR Code
- Scan the QR code by holding your device steady and aligning it in the center of the frame.
- Tap the notification or link when it appears on your screen.

Step 3: Tap the Link to Open Google Maps
- The QR code will redirect you to a Google Maps page with pinned locations for hotels and museums in Interlaken.
- You'll see detailed addresses, names, and proximity to key landmarks.

Step 4: Select Your Destination
- Select from the pinned locations on the map.
- Tap your preferred option for full details.

Step 5: Get Directions Instantly
- Tap the "Directions" button.
- Select your preferred travel mode: walking, driving, cycling, or public transportation.
- Google Maps will generate the best route with estimated time and distance

INTRODUCTION TO INTERLAKEN

I have visited alpine towns across Europe, but Interlaken holds a unique place. It is not only a destination—it is a gateway. Nestled between Lake Thun and Lake Brienz, and framed by the towering peaks of the Eiger, Mönch, and Jungfrau, this town acts as the starting point for some of Switzerland's most iconic journeys. Within minutes, I can stand before the roaring Staubbach Falls in Lauterbrunnen, ride the funicular up to Harder Kulm for sweeping views, or board a boat bound for historic lakeside villages.

Interlaken is not about staying in one spot—it is about access. Rail lines, cable cars, hiking trails, and cruise boats radiate outward like spokes on a wheel, giving travelers unmatched flexibility. Whether you chase glaciers at the Jungfraujoch, stroll quiet lakeshores, or explore alpine valleys, Interlaken keeps every path within reach.

Welcome to the Bernese Oberland

Interlaken is situated in the Bernese Oberland, a region renowned for its lakes, peaks, and valleys. The town lies between Lake Thun and Lake Brienz, with the Aare River flowing through its center. This location gives Interlaken its name: "between the lakes."

The town has two main rail stations:

- **Interlaken Ost (East)** – Untere Bönigstrasse 5, 3800 Interlaken, Switzerland [46.69042, 7.86903]

- **Interlaken West** – Bahnhofstrasse 28, 3800 Interlaken, Switzerland [46.68345, 7.85266]

Interlaken Ost is the true hub. From here, I board the Bernese Oberland Railway to Lauterbrunnen and Grindelwald, or connect to boats on Lake Brienz. Within minutes, I can switch from a train platform to a pier.

Walking along Höheweg, the main promenade, I always stop at Höhematte Park, where paragliders land throughout the day. The grand Victoria-Jungfrau Hotel, Höheweg 41 [46.68635, 7.85774], overlooks this park and symbolizes Interlaken's long tradition of hospitality.

A Brief History of Interlaken

Interlaken began as a monastic settlement in the 12th century. For centuries, it was known more for its religious significance than for tourism. That changed in the 19th century, when the rise of rail and steamships opened the area to travelers from across Europe. Grand hotels emerged, offering stunning lake views and convenient mountain access.

The layout of the town reflects this history. Boat piers align with train platforms. The flow of visitors was carefully designed to move seamlessly between modes of travel. Today, the same system serves modern travelers—efficient, punctual, and reliable.

Cultural Insights and Alpine Traditions

Life here blends modern tourism with strong alpine traditions. Respect is central:

- Always greet drivers, shopkeepers, and fellow hikers with a warm *'Grüezi'*.
- Close every pasture gate you pass.
- Keep noise low on early trains and evening walks.
- Sort waste—there are separate bins for PET, glass, paper, and organics.

Food culture reflects the highlands. I recommend trying:

- **Rösti** – crisp potato dish
- **Fondue** – melted cheese with bread
- **Älplermagronen** – Alpine macaroni with cheese and onions
- **Meiringen meringues** – a sweet invented nearby

Markets open early, bakeries even earlier, and café terraces stay lively until late summer evenings.

Why Choose This Base

I use Interlaken as my base because it gives maximum flexibility. From here:

- The Harder Kulm Funicular (Harderstrasse 34, 3800 Interlaken [46.68953, 7.85721]) lifts me to 1,322 m in just 10 minutes. The Two Lakes Bridge at the summit offers a view of both lakes simultaneously.
- Boats on Lake Thun and Lake Brienz leave from piers within walking distance.
- Day trips to Grindelwald, Lauterbrunnen, Mürren, and Wengen take less than 40 minutes.
- Scenic trains such as the GoldenPass Express connect me to Montreux on Lake Geneva.

On calm days, I stroll at Neuhaus Strandbad, Seestrasse 121, 3800 Unterseen [46.67786, 7.81691]. This lakeside area is perfect for quiet swimming and flat walking paths. On wet days, I head to St. Beatus Caves, Staatsstrasse 30, 3800 Sundlauenen [46.68431, 7.78172], where underground chambers and waterfalls keep me busy for hours.

Best Time to Visit

Interlaken works year-round, but the experience changes:

- **Late May to October** – Boats, ridge hikes, alpine gardens. Long daylight hours. Best time for first-time visitors.
- **July–August** – Peak crowds. I start days before 09:00 to avoid queues.
- **December to March** – Snow sports in Grindelwald and Mürren. Interlaken itself is not a ski resort, but it does offer sledging and winter trails.
- **April and November** – Shoulder months. Some lifts and boats pause. Suitable for quiet visits, but with limited access to high-altitude routes.

Weather rule: Strong winds close gondolas faster than snowstorms. Always check updates and prepare a backup option.

How to Get There

I reach Interlaken easily by train from Swiss airports:

- Zürich Airport → 2h20m (1 change in Bern)
- Basel Airport → 2h30m (via Basel SBB and Bern)
- Geneva Airport → 3h15m (2 changes via Bern)

Local travel is equally simple.

- **Interlaken Ost** serves as the hub for Harder Kulm, Lake Brienz boats, and the Jungfrau railways.
- **Interlaken West** serves Lake Thun cruises and town walks.
- Station lockers hold bags securely if you want to explore before check-in.

Pass Tip: If you plan to ride multiple lifts and boats, the Jungfrau Travel Pass often saves CHF 50–100 over separate tickets and skips daily queues.

My Arrival Routine

When I arrive, I follow a simple pattern:

1. Drop my bag at **Interlaken Ost lockers**.
2. Ride the **Harderbahn Funicular** for a first view.
3. Stroll down **Höheweg** for orientation.
4. Dinner either at Coop Restaurant Interlaken Ost, Untere Bönigstrasse 10 [46.68988, 7.86943] for budget efficiency, or at Victoria-Jungfrau terrace for a splurge.

This routine resets me after travel and reminds me why Interlaken remains the best base in the Swiss Alps.

CHAPTER 1: ESSENTIAL TRAVEL INFORMATION

Traveling to Interlaken is straightforward, but planning ahead ensures you avoid delays and make the most of your time in the Jungfrau region. This chapter provides the essential knowledge I've gained over multiple trips—everything from entry rules to transport passes—so you begin your journey with confidence.

Entry, Visas, and Travel Documents

Switzerland is part of the Schengen Area, which means that visitors from most European countries, the United States, Canada, Australia, New Zealand, Japan, South Korea, and several other countries can stay for up to 90 days within a 180-day period without a visa.

- **Passport Validity:** Ensure your passport is valid for at least three months beyond your intended departure date; I recommend six months to avoid potential issues.

- **Border Checks:** Although Switzerland has open borders with its EU neighbors, random spot checks are conducted. Always carry your passport or a valid national ID.

- **Extended Stay:** If you plan to stay longer or study/work, you must arrange a visa or permit in advance through the Swiss consulate in your home country.

I carry a printed copy of my hotel reservation and return flight ticket. On one occasion, I was asked to provide proof of onward travel when entering Switzerland from Germany at Basel station.

Money, Cards, and Payments

Switzerland uses the Swiss franc (CHF). Euros are sometimes accepted in tourist zones, but usually at a poor exchange rate.

- **ATMs:** Widely available at train stations (Interlaken Ost and Interlaken West), banks, and supermarkets.

- **Cards:** Visa, Mastercard, and increasingly American Express are accepted everywhere—from luxury hotels to mountain huts.

- **Mobile Payments:** Apple Pay, Google Pay, and TWINT (local Swiss app) are common.

- **Cash Tips:** Rounding up bills or leaving 5–10 CHF is appreciated. Service charges are already included in restaurant bills.

I usually withdraw CHF 100–200 at Raiffeisen Bank, Höheweg 95 (46.6858, 7.8564), then keep coins for lockers, vending machines, and luggage storage.

Safety Tips and Emergency Information

Interlaken is safe, but the mountains demand caution.

- **Emergency Numbers:** Police 117, Ambulance 144, Fire 118, Mountain Rescue 1414.
- **Weather:** Mountain conditions change in minutes. Always check the MeteoSwiss app.
- **Hiking Safety:** Pack layered clothing, a headlamp, water, and a first aid kit.
- **Insurance:** Ensure your travel insurance covers mountain rescue and helicopter evacuation.

Once, a sudden fog closed in during a hike near Männlichen. Because I had downloaded the trail map and carried a GPS-enabled phone, I safely navigated back.

Local Customs and Etiquette

- **Trains:** Keep conversations quiet, especially in "quiet zones."
- **Restaurants:** Please wait to be seated unless otherwise indicated. Payment is usually at the table.
- **Tipping:** Modest rounding up is enough.
- **Hiking Trails:** Always yield to uphill hikers. Close gates behind you when crossing pastures.
- **Shoes:** Remove hiking boots in huts; slippers are often provided.

These small gestures show respect and earn friendliness from locals.

Health Care and Pharmacies

- **Hospitals:** Interlaken Hospital, Spitalstrasse 50 (46.6841, 7.8610), provides emergency services.
- **Pharmacies:** Paracelsus Apotheke, Höheweg 47 (46.6863, 7.8578), is reliable for medicines and hiking supplies.

- **Emergency Care:** Walk-in services are available, but outside regular hours, please use the emergency line at 144.
- **Water:** Tap water is safe, often sourced directly from mountain springs.

Travel Passes and Reservations

Several passes simplify transport:

- **Swiss Travel Pass:** Unlimited travel on the SBB network, boats, and museums. Ideal for multi-city trips.
- **Jungfrau Travel Pass:** Covers Interlaken–Jungfraujoch region for 3–8 consecutive days. Best for local explorations.
- **Regional Pass Bernese Oberland:** Includes trains, boats, and buses across a wider area.

Reservations:

- Required for Jungfraujoch and scenic routes like the GoldenPass Express.
- Not required for local trains, but I recommend booking during July and August when seats fill up quickly.

I once saved over CHF 70 in two days by using the Jungfrau Travel Pass, which combines rail, bus, and mountain lift services.

Final Note

Prepared travelers enjoy Interlaken more fully. With your documents, transport, safety plan, and local customs in hand, you step into the region ready for the adventures that follow.

CHAPTER 2: TRANSPORTATION & GETTING AROUND INTERLAKEN

Nestled between Lake Thun (46.7175° N, 7.6294° E) and Lake Brienz (46.7570° N, 8.0300° E), Interlaken is the gateway to the Bernese Oberland and one of Switzerland's best-connected hubs. Over several trips, I've explored every possible route to and around this alpine paradise—by train, car, boat, cable car, and even paragliding. Whether you're arriving for a short getaway or using Interlaken as a base for the Jungfrau region, this chapter provides a complete, step-by-step guide to transportation so you can move confidently, save time, and maximize your experience.

How to Get to Interlaken

By Train — The Scenic and Stress-Free Choice
Switzerland's SBB railway network connects Interlaken seamlessly with major cities:

- **Zurich Airport (ZRH)** → Interlaken Ost (≈2 hours 10 minutes)
- **Geneva Airport (GVA)** → Interlaken Ost (≈3 hours)
- **Bern** → Interlaken Ost (≈50 minutes)
- **Lucerne** → Interlaken Ost (≈2 hours, via the Luzern–Interlaken Express)

The town has two main stations:
- **Interlaken Ost (East Station)** (Höheweg 115, 3800 Interlaken; 46.6912° N, 7.8690° E) — best for reaching Jungfraujoch, Lauterbrunnen, and Grindelwald.
- **Interlaken West (West Station)** (Bahnhofstrasse 28, 3800 Interlaken; 46.6821° N, 7.8526° E) — closer to the town center, hotels, and shopping areas.

Insider Tip: For the best scenic views, reserve window seats on the Luzern–Interlaken Express. Trains can be busy in high season, so book early to secure your spot and enjoy the ride through alpine valleys, lakes, and chalets.

By Car — Flexibility and Freedom
Driving to Interlaken gives you access to remote villages and hidden trails.
- From **Zurich**: ≈2 hours via the **A8 motorway**
- From **Geneva**: ≈3 hours via **A1 and A8 motorways**
- From **Milan, Italy**: ≈3.5 hours via **E35 motorway**

Parking Options:
- **Parking Interlaken Ost** (Lindenallee 2; 46.6915° N, 7.8702° E) — ideal for train day trips.
- **Casino Interlaken Parking** (Höheweg 31; 46.6878° N, 7.8627° E) — central and convenient.

Driving Rules:
- **Motorway vignette** required (CHF 40/year).
- Speed limits: 50 km/h (urban), 80 km/h (rural), 120 km/h (highways).
- Winter tires are recommended from November to March.

By Air — Gateway Airports

Interlaken does not have its own airport, but three international options are nearby: **Zurich Airport (ZRH)** — best for global arrivals.

- **Geneva Airport (GVA)** — ideal for combining with a visit to Lake Geneva.
- **EuroAirport Basel (BSL)** serves as a hub for regional European flights.

Each airport connects directly to Interlaken by SBB train, ensuring a seamless arrival.

Navigating Interlaken Town

Interlaken is compact and walkable, but public transport expands your reach.

Buses

Local buses link Interlaken West and Ost with major attractions, hotels, and lake promenades.

- **Bus Line 103** — connects Interlaken to Unterseen.
- **Bus Line 105** — heads towards Beatenberg and St. Beatus Caves (46.6872° N, 7.7907° E).

Purchase bus tickets at machines, through the SBB Mobile app, or directly from the driver. For convenience and savings, consider purchasing day passes if you plan to take multiple rides.

Funiculars & Cable Cars

Interlaken is surrounded by summits accessible via scenic lifts:

- **Harderbahn Funicular** (Brienzerstrasse 2; 46.6898° N, 7.8601° E) → **Harder Kulm** (10 minutes)
- **Schynige Platte Bahn** (Wilderswil; 46.6627° N, 7.8673° E) → alpine hiking paradise (50 minutes).
- **Niederhorn Cable Car** (Seestrasse 370; 46.7073° N, 7.7929° E) → stunning Lake Thun panoramas.

Ferries on Lake Thun & Lake Brienz

Seasonal ferries are a must-do for relaxed sightseeing:

- **Interlaken West Pier → Thun** (1 hour 45 minutes).

- **Interlaken Ost Pier** → **Brienz** (1 hour 20 minutes).

Tip: Combine ferries with regional trains for a scenic and cost-efficient circular route. Check schedules in advance to coordinate connections, especially in peak seasons.

Swiss Travel Pass & Regional Tickets

For multi-day trips, the Swiss Travel Pass is unbeatable:
- Unlimited rides on trains, buses, and boats.
- Free entry to 500+ museums.
- Discounts on cable cars and mountain railways.

If you plan to focus on the Jungfrau region, opt for the Jungfrau Travel Pass:
- Covers Lauterbrunnen, Grindelwald, Wengen, Mürren, Kleine Scheidegg, and beyond.
- Includes discounted trips to Jungfraujoch.

Insider Tips for Efficient Travel

- Download the SBB Mobile app for real-time schedules, digital tickets, and travel updates. This helps you adjust plans quickly if your schedule changes.
- Always check weather conditions via MeteoSwiss before heading to mountain summits.
- Reserve panoramic trains, such as the Luzern–Interlaken Express, early in the summer.
- If traveling in winter, confirm lift schedules as closures are common during heavy snowfall.

Conclusion

Moving around Interlaken isn't just about getting from A to B—it's about enjoying the journey. Use apps in advance to check the weather and reserve seats on panoramic trains, making your travel seamless. Every route offers breathtaking views, so with thoughtful planning, your trip will be both efficient and memorable.

CHAPTER 3: WHERE TO STAY IN INTERLAKEN

Choosing where to stay in Interlaken shapes your entire experience in this alpine paradise. Over the years, I've spent countless nights exploring different corners of the town—sleeping in luxury resorts with panoramic views, cozying up in boutique hotels, and even staying in rustic lakeside chalets tucked away in serene alpine settings. Interlaken's accommodation scene is wonderfully diverse, catering to every style of traveler and every budget. In this chapter, I'll walk you through the best options, complete with recommendations, addresses, insider tips, and booking strategies to help you find the perfect stay.

Luxury Hotels & Grand Resorts

(5-star retreats with spa, wellness, and alpine views)
If you want to wake up to breathtaking views of the Eiger, Mönch, and Jungfrau peaks, Interlaken offers some of Switzerland's most luxurious

alpine resorts. These stays combine world-class hospitality, fine dining, and wellness experiences designed for ultimate relaxation.

- **Victoria-Jungfrau Grand Hotel & Spa**
  Höheweg 41, 3800 Interlaken
  (46.6855° N, 7.8573° E)
  A timeless 5-star icon, featuring elegant suites, an award-winning spa, and Michelin-starred dining. It's ideal for travelers seeking privacy, sophistication, and personalized service.
- **Lindner Grand Hotel Beau Rivage**
  Höheweg 211, 3800 Interlaken
  (46.6923° N, 7.8691° E)
  Known for its Belle Époque charm, this hotel offers river-facing suites, indoor pools, and easy access to Interlaken Ost Station, making it an ideal base for day trips to Jungfraujoch.

Insider Tip: Book early during the summer season (June to August) to secure balcony rooms with mountain views.

Boutique Hotels & Alpine Charm
(Personalized stays with unique interiors)
For travelers who prefer intimate spaces and curated experiences, Interlaken's boutique hotels provide cozy stays infused with Swiss alpine character.

- **Hotel Interlaken**
  Höheweg 74, 3800 Interlaken
  (46.6887° N, 7.8659° E)
  One of Interlaken's oldest hotels, offering a tranquil garden, wood-beamed interiors, and a blend of tradition and modern comfort.
- **The Hey Hotel**
  Höheweg 7, 3800 Interlaken
  (46.6826° N, 7.8492° E)
  Perfect for younger travelers, this stylish hotel combines contemporary design with vibrant energy, featuring open lounges and social spaces.

Insider Tip: Many boutique hotels offer complimentary Interlaken Guest Cards, which provide unlimited bus rides and discounts on local activities.

Budget-Friendly Options & Hostels
(Affordable stays for backpackers and solo travelers)
Interlaken has long been a hotspot for backpackers exploring the Bernese Oberland. Affordable hostels and budget hotels make it possible to enjoy the region without overspending.

Balmer's Hostel: Hauptstrasse 23-25, 3800 Matten bei Interlaken (46.6813° N, 7.8618° E)
Switzerland's oldest private hostel, offering dorms, cozy lounges, and a vibrant nightlife scene.

Backpackers Villa Sonnenhof: Alpenstrasse 16, 3800 Interlaken (46.6845° N, 7.8596° E)
Offers spotless facilities, free breakfast, and a relaxed, communal vibe—great for meeting other travelers.

Budget Tip: Consider shared dorms to save on costs, especially during peak hiking season.

Lakeside Chalets & Mountain Lodges
(Immersive nature retreats)
If you dream of waking up to the sound of birdsong, crisp mountain air, and lake views, these chalets and lodges deliver exactly that.

- **Iseltwald Lakeside Chalet**
  Seestrasse 35, 3807 Iseltwald
  (46.7119° N, 7.9675° E)
  Nestled on the shores of Lake Brienz, this chalet offers private terraces and direct access to the lake for kayaking or morning swims.
- **Balmers Tent Village** (Summer-only)
  Hauptstrasse 23, 3800 Matten bei Interlaken
  (46.6807° N, 7.8602° E)
  A laid-back outdoor stay with tents, hammocks, and a campfire vibe, ideal for nature lovers.

Nature Tip: For the best sunrise views, opt for lodges that face the Jungfrau massif.

Family-Friendly Stays
(Spacious rooms, playgrounds, and convenient amenities)
Interlaken is ideal for families, with hotels offering spacious suites, indoor pools, and kid-friendly amenities.

- **Hotel Beausite**
  Seestrasse 16, 3800 Interlaken
  (46.6822° N, 7.8505° E)
  A charming hotel with family suites, free breakfast, and an outdoor play area for kids.
- **Hotel Du Nord**
  Höheweg 70, 3800 Interlaken
  (46.6885° N, 7.8657° E)
  Centrally located with spacious rooms and excellent proximity to Harder Kulm Funicular and local parks.

Booking Tips & Peak Season Strategies

- **Book Early:** For the summer (June–August) and ski seasons (December–February), reservations should be made 3–4 months in advance.
- **Stay Flexible:** Consider nearby villages like Wilderswil or Iseltwald for quieter stays and better rates.
- **Compare Platforms:** Use **Booking.com**, Hotels.com, and SwissTravelSystem.com to compare prices and availability.
- **Leverage Guest Cards:** Many hotels offer complimentary Interlaken Guest Cards, providing discounts on local attractions and free public transportation.

From grand resorts overlooking snow-capped peaks to hidden chalets beside turquoise lakes, Interlaken offers something for every traveler. Whether you're seeking luxury, comfort, affordability, or adventure, the right stay can transform your experience. My advice? Choose based on the kind of journey you want—relaxation, exploration, or immersion—and let your accommodation become part of the story.

CHAPTER 4: TOP ATTRACTIONS IN AND AROUND INTERLAKEN

Interlaken is more than a resort town—it is a natural base camp for some of Switzerland's most iconic alpine experiences. From panoramic peaks to tranquil cruises, each attraction offers something distinct. Below is my personal record of the places I returned to again and again, with the details you need to plan your own route.

Harder Kulm Panorama

Whenever I arrive in Interlaken, my first stop is Harder Kulm. Known as the "Top of Interlaken," it offers a complete view of Lakes Thun and Brienz with the Eiger, Mönch, and Jungfrau rising in the distance. The Harderbahn funicular leaves from Harderbahnstrasse 4, 3800 Interlaken (GPS: 46.6906° N, 7.8682° E). In ten minutes, it climbs to 1,322 meters, where a panorama platform juts into the air. From there, you see how Interlaken rests like a bridge between two lakes. I recommend visiting in the late afternoon, staying until sunset, and having dinner at the Harder Kulm restaurant located beside the platform. It is an easy, rewarding excursion for your first day in town.

Jungfraujoch – Top of Europe

No journey through Interlaken is complete without the train to Jungfraujoch. Standing at 3,454 meters, it is the highest railway station in Europe. The route begins in Interlaken Ost (GPS: 46.6913° N, 7.8699° E), with connections through Lauterbrunnen or Grindelwald. The ride itself feels like an ascent into another world: glaciers, tunnels carved through rock, and windows framing snowfields. At the summit, I walked through the Ice Palace, stepped onto the viewing terrace, and felt the thin air as I looked across the Aletsch Glacier. Tickets are costly, but worth every franc if you want one Alpine experience that defines Switzerland. Go early, check weather updates, and bring layers.

Schilthorn – Piz Gloria

High above Mürren lies the Schilthorn, famous not just for its 2,970-meter views but also as the setting of the James Bond film *On Her Majesty's Secret Service*. To reach it, I took the cable car sequence from Stechelberg (GPS: 46.5580° N, 7.9107° E) via Gimmelwald and Mürren. At the summit, the revolving restaurant Piz Gloria slowly revealed peaks in every direction, including the jagged Eiger. I tried their Bond-themed brunch while the panorama turned like a slow carousel. The thrill here is both cinematic and natural: standing on the observation deck with mountains filling the horizon. For me, Schilthorn felt less crowded than Jungfraujoch but no less dramatic.

Lauterbrunnen Valley and Waterfalls

The Lauterbrunnen Valley is one of those places that humbles you. A glacial trough lined with sheer cliffs, it holds 72 waterfalls. From Interlaken Ost, trains run directly to Lauterbrunnen village (GPS: 46.5931° N, 7.9070° E). The moment you step off the platform, Staubbach Falls pours down in front of you. I walked the valley floor, where alpine houses rest below constant curtains of water. Each bend offered another waterfall tumbling from impossible heights. Buses and cable cars link to Wengen, Mürren, and Grütschalp, but I often prefer simply walking the valley path. The sound of rushing water follows you everywhere.

Trümmelbach and Staubbach Falls

Within Lauterbrunnen Valley lie two of the most striking falls. Staubbach, visible from the village, is best visited in the morning when sunlight catches the mist. A short uphill path leads to a gallery behind the cascade. A few kilometers deeper into the valley, the Trümmelbach Falls (GPS: 46.5624° N, 7.9108° E) roar inside the mountain itself. Ten glacial waterfalls rush through tunnels and chambers, accessible by a lift and walkways. The sound is deafening, the power almost overwhelming. Standing in those caverns, I felt the sheer force of alpine meltwater. Both falls reveal different aspects of nature—Staubbach is graceful and open, while Trümmelbach is hidden and violent.

Schynige Platte and Alpine Garden

Schynige Platte is a nostalgic journey in itself. To reach it, I boarded the cogwheel train from Wilderswil station (GPS: 46.6645° N, 7.8662° E). The ride, dating back to 1893, is slow and steady, climbing through forests and meadows with ever-widening views of the Jungfrau massif. At 1,967 meters, the summit offers one of the most iconic panoramas in the Bernese Oberland. I followed trails that led along ridge paths where alpine flowers colored the slopes. The Alpine Garden, located near the station, is a living museum, home to over 600 plant species that thrive at this altitude. I remember pausing beside edelweiss and gentians, reading notes about how each flower has adapted to harsh alpine conditions. Families will enjoy the gentle hikes, while seasoned hikers can push toward Faulhorn for even grander views. Whenever I visit, I feel like I've stepped into a Swiss postcard that moves slowly, letting every detail settle in.

Grindelwald First and Bachalpsee

Grindelwald First is where adventure meets scenery. From the village of Grindelwald (GPS: 46.6240° N, 8.0414° E), the gondola rises to First in about 25 minutes. At the top, a suspension walkway, called the First Cliff Walk by Tissot, clings dramatically to the cliff face, ending with a platform that juts out into the air. I stood there with nothing but sky and peaks before me. First, the most beloved hike is the 50-minute trail to Bachalpsee, a serene alpine lake at 2,265 meters. On a clear day, its waters reflect the Wetterhorn and Schreckhorn peaks, making it one of the most photographed spots in Switzerland. I carried a picnic, sat at the lake's edge, and watched clouds drift across mirrored peaks. For thrill-seekers, First offers a zip line, mountain carts, and trotti-bikes that speed down to the valley. Whether for calm reflection at Bachalpsee or adrenaline rides, Grindelwald First rewards every traveler with a taste of the high Alps.

Brienz Rothorn Railway

The Brienz Rothorn Railway is a time machine powered by steam. Departing from Brienz station (GPS: 46.7553° N, 8.0386° E), this cogwheel train climbs 7.6 kilometers to Rothorn Kulm at 2,244 meters. The carriages are open, and the scent of coal mixes with crisp alpine air. Built in 1892, it is Switzerland's last daily steam-powered rack railway. I remember leaning out to see the locomotive push against gravity, its black smoke trailing against the blue sky. At the summit, the panorama opens toward the Brienzersee below and a jagged horizon of peaks stretching into central Switzerland. Trails branch out from Rothorn, but I found joy simply sitting at the summit restaurant terrace, watching steam engines arrive like living relics. For me, this journey is less about speed and more about savoring each ascent, each curve, and each whistle echoing off the mountainsides. If you want to experience travel as it was over a century ago, this is the place to be.

St. Beatus Caves

Legends and geology meet at the St. Beatus Caves, tucked above Lake Thun (GPS: 46.7001° N, 7.7789° E). Folklore claims a monk named Beatus drove out a dragon here in the 6th century. Today, you walk through illuminated chambers carved by water over millions of years. Stalactites hang like frozen curtains, and underground streams flow beneath the walkways. I took the guided tour, which lasts approximately 75 minutes, and found it to be both scientific and mystical. Outside, a small museum explains the cave's geology, while terraces above the entrance offer grand views of Lake Thun. The walk up from the parking area is steep but scenic, passing waterfalls and forest paths. Dining at the cave restaurant afterward, with the lake glittering below, is part of the reward. I left with the feeling of stepping out of myth into sunlight. For families, this site combines story, nature, and spectacle in a single, unforgettable experience.

Giessbach Falls and Grandhotel Giessbach

Few places combine natural spectacle and historic charm like Giessbach Falls. Located on the southern shore of Lake Brienz (GPS: 46.7414° N, 8.0337° E), the waterfalls tumble over 14 tiers before crashing into the lake. I approached via the Giessbach funicular, the oldest of its kind in Europe, which still carries visitors from the boat landing up to the Grandhotel Giessbach. Built in 1875, the hotel feels like stepping into the Belle Époque era: wooden balconies, chandeliers, and terraces overlooking the roaring falls. Walking the forest paths around the cascades, I passed viewpoints where the spray cooled my face and rainbows arched in the mist. At night, the falls are illuminated, adding a dreamlike aura. I stayed for coffee on the hotel terrace, where the thundering water became a soundtrack to quiet elegance. This combination of raw alpine energy and refined hospitality is uniquely Swiss, and I never leave without feeling both refreshed and a sense of nostalgia.

Lake Thun Cruise

Lake Thun stretches like a blue corridor between Thun and Interlaken, framed by castles, vineyards, and alpine ridges. I boarded the boat at Interlaken West (GPS: 46.6805° N, 7.8529° E), where modern vessels glide as smoothly as floating balconies. The full cruise to Thun takes approximately two hours, stopping at lakeside villages such as Spiez, featuring its castle and wine terraces. On deck, the breeze carried scents of pine and water, while the Eiger, Mönch, and Jungfrau formed a distant backdrop. The boat itself felt like part café, part moving theater, with open-air seating and large panoramic windows. I ordered rösti from the onboard restaurant and ate while the shoreline unfolded like chapters of a storybook. The lake is especially magical in the evening, when the setting sun bathes castles like Oberhofen in amber light. For me, this cruise is more than transport—it is a way to see the Oberland at a gentler pace, one shoreline at a time.

Lake Brienz Cruise

Lake Brienz, with its turquoise waters, feels more dramatic and secluded than Lake Thun. From Interlaken Ost (GPS: 46.6906° N, 7.8680° E), I boarded a vintage paddle steamer whose wooden decks and brass fittings echo the 19th century. The cruise winds past sheer cliffs, forests, and villages, such as Iseltwald, a fishing hamlet where time seems to stand still. Along the eastern shore lies the Giessbach stop, where passengers step off to ride the funicular to the waterfalls and hotel. I recall leaning over the rail to watch the water shimmer in impossible shades of blue-green, shifting with every angle of the sun. On quieter stretches, it felt like sailing through a fjord. The crew serves regional wines and snacks, and I always recommend taking at least part of the trip on deck. On a clear morning, the stillness of Lake Brienz mirrors every peak above, making the journey itself a work of art.

Niederhorn Summit Views

The Niederhorn is a summit where the Alps meet calm observation. To reach it, I traveled by funicular from Beatenbucht to Beatenberg (GPS: 46.7007° N, 7.7953° E), then switched to a cable car that swung upward with sweeping views of Lake Thun. At 1,963 meters, the summit reveals both the Bernese Alps and the long ridges of the Jura in the distance. I joined a short walk along the ridge, where marmots sometimes pop out from burrows and ibex graze the slopes. Families often choose the easy stroller-friendly paths, while hikers can push toward Burgfeldstand for sharper panoramas. In winter, Niederhorn becomes a ski and sledding area, less crowded than Grindelwald or Wengen. I once stayed until evening and watched the light fade across Lake Thun—a slow theatre of color that felt unhurried. For travelers seeking altitude without crowds, Niederhorn is a steady favorite.

Ballenberg Open-Air Museum

Ballenberg is less about peaks and more about Switzerland's living heritage. Located near Brienz (GPS: 46.7514° N, 8.0376° E), this open-air museum spreads across 66 hectares of meadows and forests. Over 100 historic farmhouses, barns, and workshops from every Swiss canton have been rebuilt here. Walking the grounds felt like crossing centuries: wooden chalets with carved balconies from Bern, stone houses from Ticino, and alpine huts where cheese was once made. Artisans demonstrate blacksmithing, weaving, and bread baking, and I often linger to watch the rhythm of old tools at work. Farm animals graze nearby, providing families with numerous interaction points. The museum changes with the seasons—spring flowers surround the farmsteads, autumn harvest festivals, and craft fairs are held throughout the year. I carried a notebook and kept writing down how daily life once pulsed in these walls. Ballenberg is not a static museum; it is a living landscape of tradition.

Thun Old Town and Castles

At the western edge of Lake Thun, the town of Thun (GPS: 46.7570° N, 7.6278° E) blends lake life with medieval charm. I walked through cobbled streets where raised sidewalks give unique double-level access to shops and cafés. Dominating the skyline is Thun Castle, built in the 12th century, with four white towers that rise like sentinels. The climb up rewards with views over the old town's red roofs and the lake stretching toward Interlaken. Nearby, the Schadau Castle, set within a lakeside park, is smaller but refined, housing a gastronomy museum and restaurant. My favorite memory was an afternoon stroll along the Aare riverbanks, where I watched locals paddle canoes and children feed swans. Thun's blend of castle history, riverside charm, and modern cafés makes it an essential bookend to an Interlaken stay. Unlike the tourist hubs, this is a lived-in Swiss city with a gentle pace.

Tourismuseum Interlaken

Tourismuseum Interlaken is Switzerland's first museum dedicated entirely to the history of Alpine tourism, located in Unterseen's charming Old Town. Housed in a beautifully preserved 17th-century timbered building, it offers a fascinating journey through over 500 years of tourism development in the Jungfrau region. Visitors can explore three floors of exhibits featuring vintage skis, steamship and railway models, postcards, hotel memorabilia, and interactive displays like "The Tourism Game." Situated at Obere Gasse 26, 3800 Unterseen (GPS: 46.68695° N, 7.84919° E), the museum is open Wednesday to Sunday, 2:00 PM – 5:00 PM. Perfect for history lovers and curious travelers, it highlights how Interlaken evolved into one of Switzerland's most iconic destinations.

The Monastery and Interlaken Castle

The Monastery and Interlaken Castle, dating to 1133, sit between Höhematte Park and the Japanese Garden. Founded by Baron Seliger of Oberhofen as an Augustinian monastery, it once housed both male and female religious communities. After the Reformation (1525–1528), the state of Bern repurposed it into a hospital, administrative center, and granary. Today, several medieval features remain, including the 14th-century church tower, the 1452 Gothic cloister gallery, and a peaceful chapel. The castle grounds are open to the public year-round, offering shaded paths and benches ideal for quiet reflection. Its blend of spiritual heritage and civic history makes it one of Interlaken's most fascinating sites, perfect for travelers interested in architecture, culture, and centuries-old traditions.

CHAPTER 5: LOCAL CUISINE IN INTERLAKEN

When people think of Interlaken, they imagine peaks, lakes, and cable cars. Yet the region's cuisine is just as important to the travel experience as its landscapes. Meals in the Bernese Oberland are hearty, built for long days outdoors, and shaped by centuries of Alpine farming traditions. Cheese from mountain dairies, potatoes stored through winter, and smoked meats cured for survival are the foundation of the dishes you find on local menus today. Eating here is not only about satisfying hunger but also about connecting with the rhythms of mountain life.

Must-Try Dishes of the Bernese Oberland

Rösti
Rösti is often described as the national dish of Switzerland, and in Interlaken, it holds a place of honor. This golden potato pancake began as a

farmer's breakfast in Bern, made to fuel long hours in the fields. Today it is served at all hours, sometimes plain, sometimes with toppings like fried eggs, mountain cheese, ham, or sautéed onions. Each region prepares it differently, but in Interlaken, you will often see rösti cooked in individual pans, ensuring a crisp edge and a soft center. At Gasthof Hirschen (Höheweg 115, 3800 Interlaken, 46.6866° N, 7.8566° E), the rösti comes to the table in a sizzling skillet, a portion large enough to share after a day of hiking. Locals treat it as comfort food, pairing it with a Rugenbräu beer or a glass of white wine. For travelers, rösti is more than a side dish—it is an introduction to Swiss Alpine simplicity, proof that potatoes, when treated with care, can carry the weight of tradition.

Fondue

Few meals embody the spirit of Swiss dining like fondue. Originating as a practical way to stretch bread and cheese through the winter months, it has become a national ritual. A pot of melted Gruyère and Emmental cheese, infused with garlic and white wine, sits over a flame while diners dip bread cubes with long forks. The pace is unhurried, and the social aspect is as important as the food itself. In Interlaken, The Chalet (Höheweg 95, 3800 Interlaken,

46.6862° N, 7.8561° E) is a classic stop, its wooden interior decorated with cowbells and carvings. Tradition dictates that if you drop your bread into the pot, you owe your companions either a round of drinks or a playful forfeit. For a variation, try tomato fondue or mushroom fondue, both of which are offered in the region. Each bite reflects centuries of Alpine dairying, a communal meal designed to be eaten slowly, often lasting hours.

Raclette

Raclette takes the love of melted cheese to a new level. The name comes from the French word "racler," meaning "to scrape." A half-wheel of semi-hard raclette cheese is heated, and the bubbling layer is scraped onto boiled potatoes, pickled onions, and cornichons. The combination is rich, sharp, and filling, often eaten with dried meats and rye bread. While raclette machines are common in Swiss homes, in restaurants, the cheese is often melted at the table, adding a theatrical element to the meal. Raclette-Stube in Grindelwald (Dorfstrasse 155, 3818 Grindelwald, 46.6247° N, 8.0416° E) offers a memorable version, with staff wheeling out the cheese and serving it hot onto each plate. The smoky aroma lingers in the air, and the taste captures the essence of mountain food: simple ingredients, made indulgent through fire and patience.

Älplermagronen

Älplermagronen, sometimes called "herdsman's macaroni," is a true Alpine invention. The dish layers pasta, potatoes, cheese, cream, and onions, baked into a hearty casserole. It is typically served with a side of stewed apples, providing a sweet counterpoint to the richness of the main dish. Farmers originally prepared it in mountain huts using ingredients they had on hand: dried pasta, potatoes from storage, and cheese from their own cows. Today, it remains popular among hikers and skiers seeking comfort after exertion. One of the best places to try it is at Restaurant Harder Kulm (46.7022° N, 7.8661° E), where the view from the terrace—spanning Lake Thun, Lake Brienz, and the Jungfrau—elevates the experience. The combination of heavy food and fresh air makes this dish unforgettable.

Bernese Platte

The Bernese Platte is a feast traditionally served in winter, especially on January 5, marking the day Bernese troops returned victorious in 1798. It features an assortment of meats—smoked pork, beef, ham, sausages, and bacon—accompanied by sauerkraut, beans, and boiled potatoes. The meal is intentionally heavy, designed to feed entire groups of soldiers and families. Today it remains a symbol of regional pride. In Interlaken, the Victoria Jungfrau Grand Hotel (Höheweg 41, 3800 Interlaken, 46.6867° N,

7.8573° E) serves an elegant version, while smaller inns in nearby villages maintain the rustic, communal spirit of the dish. Eating the Bernese Platte is not only about flavor but also about history, each bite echoing a moment of resilience from Switzerland's past.

Meiringen Meringues with Cream

Meiringen, a short train ride from Interlaken, claims to be the birthplace of meringues. Legend ties their creation to an Italian chef in the 18th century, though the Swiss firmly stake their claim. Here, meringues are paired with thick double cream from local dairies, a combination that balances sweet and rich flavors. At Café Frutal (Bahnhofplatz 8, 3860 Meiringen, 46.7273° N, 8.1890° E), they are served in towering portions, often topped with fruit. For many travelers, this dessert is a highlight, both for its flavor and its cultural symbolism: a small-town specialty that has achieved global fame.

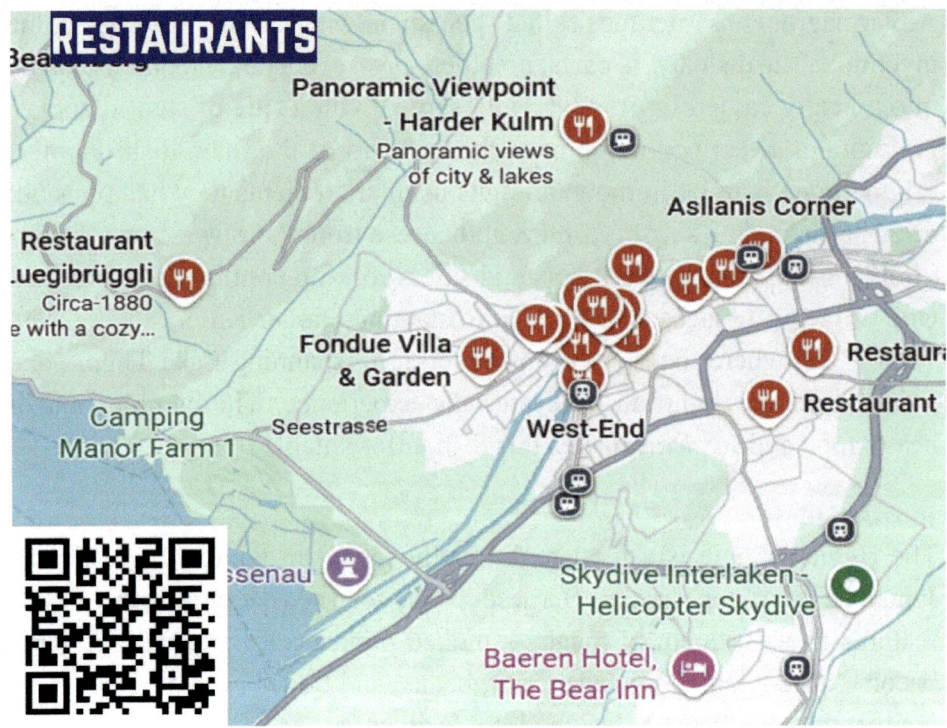

CHAPTER 6: ACTIVITIES AND EXPERIENCES

When I first arrived in Interlaken, I thought of it as a quiet alpine base. But the more I explored, the more I realized this town is an entire stage for experiences. The surrounding lakes, valleys, and peaks create a playground that changes with each season. Whether gliding across turquoise waters, climbing ridge trails, or free-falling toward emerald meadows, Interlaken has a way of turning ordinary days into unforgettable adventures. In this chapter, I share the activities that kept me coming back, each one an invitation to step outside comfort and embrace the Swiss Alps with all senses awake.

On the Water

Boat Tours, Kayaking, and SUP
There are two sides to Interlaken's waters: the relaxed drift and the active paddle. On Lake Thun (46.7357° N, 7.6200° E), I boarded a traditional paddle steamer at *Thun Schifffahrt* (Seestrasse 9, 3600 Thun). From the open deck, castles rose along the shoreline, their spires mirrored in deep-blue water. On Lake Brienz (46.7389° N, 8.0770° E), the color is startling—a turquoise glow born from glacial silt. Here I rented a kayak from *Hightide Kayak School* (Brienzstrasse 66, 3800 Bönigen). Gliding close to cliffs, I felt the stillness broken only by the dip of paddles. For a more modern thrill, stand-up paddleboarding (SUP) lets you balance against the alpine breeze. At sunrise, when the lakes are glassy, the experience feels almost meditative. Boat cruises are perfect for families or travelers who prefer comfort, while kayaking and SUP invite a more personal connection with the water's rhythm.

Fishing and Lakeside Swimming

Fishing in Interlaken is more than a sport; it is a tradition. I joined locals along the banks of Lake Brienz, where permits can be obtained from the tourist office (Marktgasse 1, 3800 Interlaken). Trout, perch, and Arctic char are common catches, and if you're lucky, you may hook a whitefish, a regional specialty. Swimming spots are plentiful: *Strandbad Thun* (Seestrasse 45, 3600 Thun) offers diving boards and grassy sunbathing lawns, while Neuhaus Beach (46.6830° N, 7.7800° E) at Lake Thun is family-friendly, with calm shallows and a small restaurant serving schnitzel and fries. I often swam here in summer evenings, when the mountains turned purple with sunset. The water, fed by glacial streams, is bracing but invigorating. In quieter corners, such as *Bönigen Lido*, the lakefront feels almost private, with a backdrop of snow-dusted ridges.

Fishing and swimming bring a slower rhythm to Interlaken, grounding you between the higher-adrenaline pursuits.

Outdoor Adventures

Hiking and Panorama Walks

No trip to Interlaken feels complete without lacing up hiking boots. Trails range from gentle lakeside strolls along turquoise waters to high ridge walks with sweeping, dizzying views of valleys. My favorite introduction is the Harder Kulm Panorama Trail (46.7023° N, 7.8667° E), accessed by funicular from Interlaken Ost (Harderbahn, Höheweg 74, 3800 Interlaken). This ridge route offers glass-floored viewpoints, benches, and uninterrupted vistas over both lakes and the Jungfrau massif. For a more immersive alpine experience, hike from Männlichen (46.6105° N, 7.9378° E) to Kleine Scheidegg—a panoramic path skirting flower-dotted meadows and passing directly beneath the Eiger's towering north face. Those seeking wildflower meadows should head to Schynige Platte, where undulating trails thread past botanical alpine gardens and echo with the gentle clang of cowbells. Maps are well-marked, and GPS coordinates included in this guide make planning simple. Whether two hours or two days, hiking here feels like a moving meditation: every step reveals dramatic, ever-changing mountain vistas.

Mountain Biking and E-Biking

The first time I pedaled out of Interlaken on two wheels, I understood why this region draws cyclists from across Europe. The network of trails is as varied as the terrain. Beginners often start with the lakeside routes—smooth, flat paths circling Lake Thun or Lake Brienz, with rest stops at villages like Spiez (46.6844° N, 7.6911° E). For more challenge, the climb toward Grindelwald (46.6242° N, 8.0423° E) is rewarded with switchbacks and sweeping glacier views.

E-bikes, widely available for rent at *Flying Wheels* (Hoeheweg 133, 3800 Interlaken), level the playing field. With a motor boost, I reached the alpine meadows of Isenfluh (46.6331° N, 7.8824° E) without feeling exhausted, leaving me with more energy to enjoy the scenery. Some routes, like the trail to Lauterbrunnen, pass through tunnels of pine forest before suddenly opening to valley floors lined with waterfalls.

Mountain bikers seeking adrenaline head to Bike Park Thunersee in Steffisburg or to the technical descents near Mürren, where rocky tracks demand their full focus. Local guides are worth hiring for advanced rides, not only for safety but also to uncover trails less known to tourists. Whether powered by pedal or e-assist, cycling through this landscape connects you directly to its rhythm—wind in your face, cowbells in the distance, and peaks rising on every horizon.

Winter Sports: Skiing, Sledging, and Snowshoeing

Winter transforms Interlaken into a basecamp for snow adventures. I often began with the short train ride to Grindelwald First or Wengen, where ski areas are linked to the Jungfrau Ski Region (46.6056° N, 7.9222° E). Together, these resorts offer over 200 km of slopes. Beginners head to *Bodmi Arena* in Grindelwald, while experts tackle the Lauberhorn Run, one of the world's longest downhill courses.

Not all winter fun requires skis. The Eiger Run Sledging Trail, stretching from Alpiglen to Grindelwald, is an exhilarating ride beneath the north face of the Eiger. I once timed my visit to coincide with the evening sledge runs, when floodlights lit the trail and the air carried the scent of mulled wine from the mountain huts.

Snowshoeing is quieter but equally rewarding. Routes above Lauterbrunnen or near Axalp (46.7280° N, 8.0465° E) cut through silent forests where the only sound is snow crunching underfoot. Equipment can be easily rented at Intersport shops throughout Interlaken. For those needing a break from action, spa hotels in Beatenberg and wellness centers in Grindelwald offer heated pools with mountain views—perfect for easing muscles after a day in the snow. Winter here strikes a balance between speed and stillness, offering every traveler a way to fully embrace the alpine season.

Paragliding and Skydiving

Every time I watch paragliders take off from Beatenberg (46.7048° N, 7.7936° E), I'm reminded why Interlaken is a global hub for aerial sports. The launch site is situated 1,350 meters above sea level, offering sweeping views of Lake Thun, Lake Brienz, and the white peaks of the Jungfrau massif. Tandem flights, offered by operators such as *Paragliding Interlaken* (Hoeheweg 115, 3800 Interlaken), run year-round. In winter, the flight is crisp and still; in summer, warm updrafts carry you higher than expected. Landings happen on a meadow beside Höhematte Park, right in the town center.

For those craving even more adrenaline, skydiving delivers. Planes take off from Reichenbach Airfield (46.6156° N, 7.6772° E), climbing to altitudes over 4,000 meters. The jump offers a heart-stopping free fall against the backdrop of the Eiger, Mönch, and Jungfrau, before the parachute slows the descent for a gentle glide into the valley. I still remember my first jump—an overwhelming mix of fear and awe that turned into pure exhilaration. Both paragliding and skydiving are tightly regulated here, with experienced pilots, modern equipment, and strong safety standards.

Canyoning and White-Water Rafting

Few experiences match the intensity of sliding, jumping, and abseiling through alpine gorges. Canyoning Grimsel, near Innertkirchen (46.7098° N, 8.2365° E), is a favorite. The granite walls, clear pools, and natural slides make it both thrilling and beautiful. Outfits like *Outdoor Interlaken* (Hauptstrasse 15, 3800 Matten) supply all gear, including wetsuits, helmets, and harnesses. I found the cold water bracing, but the rush of leaping into crystal-blue pools is unforgettable.

Rafting trips typically run on the Lütschine River, which flows from the Eiger's glaciers into Lake Brienz. The rapids here rate as Class III–IV in early summer, when snowmelt swells the river. Paddling with a group, shouting commands over the roar of water, is both demanding and exhilarating. For calmer days, rafting on the Simme River near Därstetten offers a gentler introduction. These activities are seasonal, running from May to September, and are always led by certified guides. The balance of physical challenge and alpine beauty makes canyoning and rafting standout adventures in the region.

Via Ferrata Mürren and Zipline Rides

Hanging from iron rungs bolted into cliffs above Lauterbrunnen Valley (46.5589° N, 7.8920° E), I realized how unique the Via Ferrata Mürren truly is. This fixed climbing route stretches nearly 2 km, with exposed sections crossing rope bridges and sheer drops of 600 meters. Highlights include the suspension bridge near Gimmelwald and the "Nepal Bridge," a narrow crossing that challenges even the most confident hikers. Equipment is available for rent in Mürren, but beginners are advised to consider hiring a guide for added safety. The views—valley waterfalls on one side, the Jungfrau massif on the other—reward every step.

For a different kind of thrill, zipline rides add speed to the scenery. At Grindelwald First, the "First Flyer" and "First Glider" are two of the most popular. I strapped in and shot across 800 meters of cable at speeds reaching 80 km/h, feeling the wind tear past while the valley floor stretched below. In winter, the same ride operates over snowy slopes, doubling the drama. Shorter ziplines are available at adventure parks around Interlaken, making them accessible for families as well. Both Via Ferrata and ziplines turn the mountains into playgrounds, reminding you that thrill and landscape go hand in hand here.

CHAPTER 7: ITINERARIES FOR DIFFERENT TYPES OF TRAVELERS

Whenever I return to Interlaken, I am reminded that no two travelers come here for the same reason. Some want to tick off world-famous icons like Jungfraujoch, while others chase adrenaline, seek family-friendly days, or hope to enjoy the slow rhythm of mountain life. Over the years, I've tested dozens of routes, adjusting them for time, energy, and budget. What follows are itineraries I would personally recommend, designed to help you match your stay to your travel style.

Itinerary for First-Time Visitors (3 Days)

Day 1: Town Highlights and Harder Kulm

I always begin with Interlaken itself. Start at the Höhematte Park (Höheweg 72, 3800 Interlaken, 46.6869° N, 7.8632° E), where paragliders land and the Jungfrau looms in the background. Explore Unterseen's medieval lanes before taking the Harderbahn funicular to Harder Kulm (46.7021° N, 7.8649° E). From its glass-floored viewing platform, the twin lakes shine turquoise, perfectly framing the Eiger, Mönch, and Jungfrau.

Day 2: Jungfraujoch or Schilthorn
Choose between the "Top of Europe" at Jungfraujoch (3,454 m, 46.5476° N, 7.9806° E) with its Ice Palace and glacier plateau, or the Schilthorn (2,970 m, 46.5570° N, 7.8355° E) for panoramic views immortalized in the James Bond film *On Her Majesty's Secret Service*.

Day 3: Lakes and Waterfalls
Spend a day around the lakes. A Lake Brienz cruise (departing from Interlaken Ost) pairs well with a stop at Giessbach Falls and the historic Grandhotel Giessbach (46.7471° N, 8.0330° E). Alternatively, visit Lauterbrunnen Valley's Staubbach and Trümmelbach Falls for a finale that captures Switzerland's dramatic alpine spirit.

Itinerary for Adventure Seekers (5 Days)

Day 1: Ridge Walks and Viewpoints
Start with the Schynige Platte Panorama Trail, one of my favorite ridge walks, where flower-studded meadows meet sweeping lake views.

Day 2: Paragliding or Skydiving
Launch with Interlaken's famed paragliding (often from Beatenberg, 46.7102° N, 7.7904° E) or push further with a tandem skydive above the Jungfrau massif.

Day 3: Canyoning or Rafting
In summer, canyoning through Saxeten Gorge or rafting the Lütschine River is the ultimate thrill.

Day 4: Glacier Views and Alpine Rails
Ride to Jungfraujoch or trek up to the Glacier Gorge in Grindelwald (46.6243° N, 8.0347° E).

Day 5: Hidden Valleys and Sunset Spots
Wind down in Lauterbrunnen's quieter trails or take the funicular to Niederhorn (46.7001° N, 7.7819° E) for a sunset above Lake Thun.

Itinerary for Families (4 Days)

Day 1: Easy Walks and Lake Cruise
I recommend a relaxed Lake Thun cruise, paired with gentle lakeside paths at Spiez.

Day 2: Animal Parks and Interactive Museums
Spend the day at Alpine Wildlife Park Harder (46.7024° N, 7.8652° E) or the Swiss Open-Air Museum Ballenberg (46.7434° N, 8.0380° E), where traditional farmhouses bring Swiss history to life.

Day 3: Playgrounds and Picnic Points
Children love the large play park at Mürren or the shaded riverside meadows of Lütschine Valley.

Day 4: Schynige Platte and Alpine Garden
Finish with a nostalgic cogwheel train to Schynige Platte, home to an Alpine Garden with over 600 plant species.

Itinerary for Luxury Travelers (5 Days)

Day 1: Grand Hotels and Fine Dining
Check into Victoria-Jungfrau Grand Hotel (Höheweg 41, 3800 Interlaken, 46.6866° N, 7.8620° E) before dining at La Terrasse Brasserie.

Day 2: Private Guide and Scenic Rail
Hire a local guide for a tailored experience, then ride the GoldenPass Line for a private rail journey through alpine scenery.

Day 3: Spa Day and Gourmet Tasting
Indulge in spa treatments at your hotel, then sample Swiss wines from the Lake Thun vineyards.

Day 4: Helicopter or Charter Boat
Book a helicopter flight around the Eiger or charter a private boat on Lake Brienz.

Day 5: Signature Views and Sunsets
End with champagne at Harder Kulm or a private sunset spot overlooking Lauterbrunnen Valley.

Itinerary for Return Visitors (4 Days)

Day 1: Quiet Shores and Forest Trails
Wander the Seeli at Iseltwald (46.7109° N, 7.9622° E)—a peaceful lakeside corner often overlooked.

Day 2: Lesser-Known Lifts and Ridges
Take the funicular to Allmendhubel above Mürren (46.5597° N, 7.8922° E) for alpine playgrounds and ridge trails.

Day 3: Open-Air Museums and Craft Stops
Explore Ballenberg in greater detail or visit Brienz's woodcarving workshops.

Day 4: Historic Towns and Castles
Stroll through Thun Old Town, its medieval arcades, and Thun Castle (46.7570° N, 7.6283° E), rounding out your return visit with a touch of history.

CHAPTER 8: WHAT TO DO AND WHAT NOT TO DO IN THE ALPS

Traveling through the Swiss Alps is as much about respect as it is about adventure. Interlaken and the Jungfrau region are places where the natural world and human culture coexist in a delicate balance. Over the years, I have come to realize that enjoying the mountains comes with a responsibility. These peaks are not just tourist playgrounds; they are working landscapes of farmers, climbers, and communities who have protected them for centuries. Every action we take—choosing a trail, eating in a mountain hut, or disposing of waste—leaves a mark. This chapter is my honest guide to the do's and don'ts of alpine travel, shaped by lessons learned, mistakes witnessed, and advice given by locals who call these valleys home.

What to Do

Respect Trails, Pastures, and Closures
In the Alps, every trail tells a story—one of careful planning, safety, and respect for the land. When I first hiked above Lauterbrunnen, I made the mistake of veering off a marked path to chase a "shortcut." I ended up in a farmer's pasture, face-to-face with a herd of cows and a not-so-happy farmer. Swiss trails are clearly marked with yellow signposts or red-white stripes painted on rocks and trees. Staying on them is not just about avoiding fines; it's about protecting fragile alpine meadows from erosion and safeguarding yourself against hidden hazards. Seasonal closures are also common, especially in spring when avalanches or landslides are a real risk. If a path is closed, it is for your protection. Think of trails as agreements: locals open them to us, and in return, we honor the boundaries.

Use Public Transport Smartly
One of the marvels of traveling in Switzerland is its transport system. Interlaken sits at the heart of a web of trains, boats, buses, and cable cars that connect every valley and summit. I still marvel at how easily I can board a train from Interlaken Ost (46.6867° N, 7.8632° E) and be in Lauterbrunnen in just 20 minutes, with connections to Mürren, Wengen, and Grindelwald. Using public transport not only saves you the stress of driving and parking in mountain villages, but also helps preserve these delicate regions from congestion. Passes like the Swiss Travel Pass or the Berner Oberland Regional Pass allow unlimited travel, and I've personally saved hours (and francs) by using them. Boats on Lake Brienz and Lake Thun, trams in Thun, and even funiculars like the Harderbahn are all covered. The best part? You get to sit back and enjoy alpine views instead of worrying about winding roads.

Seek Lesser-Known Viewpoints
Every visitor rushes to Jungfraujoch or Harder Kulm, and for good reason—they are spectacular. But if you stop there, you miss the Alps' quieter soul. On one visit, I chose to ride the cable car up to Niederhorn (47.7174° N, 7.7910° E), a summit overlooking Lake Thun. Instead of fighting for space

at the railing, I stood nearly alone, watching golden eagles circle in the thermals. Another time, I skipped the crowds at Staubbach Falls and walked further down the Lauterbrunnen Valley, where lesser-known cascades tumbled down sheer cliffs with no audience but myself and a few grazing cows. Seeking out these overlooked spots enriches your journey and eases pressure on the busiest attractions. A rule I follow: if you see a yellow hiking sign pointing toward a ridge or lake you haven't heard of, take it—you might discover a new favorite.

Try Regional Food and Drinks
Food is one of the most authentic windows into Alpine life. I'll never forget my first plate of rösti—crispy potatoes fried to perfection—at Restaurant Laterne (Höheweg 133, 3800 Interlaken). In winter, I shared fondue with hikers at a chalet above Grindelwald, dipping bread into bubbling cheese as the snow fell outside. Each dish carries tradition: raclette, melted over potatoes and pickles; älplermagronen, a hearty pasta with cheese and apples; or meringues from Meiringen (46.7276° N, 8.1832° E), the birthplace of this sweet treat. Drinks are equally important—local wines from the Valais, or a cold Rugenbräu beer brewed right in Interlaken. Eating and drinking locally does more than fill you up—it supports farmers, keeps traditions alive, and gives you memories that postcards cannot.

Support Local Makers
Markets in towns like Brienz and Thun reveal the true heartbeat of the region. I once bought a hand-carved wooden cow in Brienz from a craftsman whose family had worked with wood for four generations. It cost more than a plastic souvenir, but it sits on my desk as a lasting reminder of place and craft. Supporting local makers—whether by purchasing cheese at the Alpine market in Interlaken, handmade textiles in Lauterbrunnen, or art in Grindelwald—ensures your spending directly benefits the community. It also resists the homogenization of tourism. When you carry home something unique and handcrafted, you carry home a story that continues long after you leave.

What Not to Do

Disturb Wildlife or Pick Protected Flowers

Edelweiss, gentians, and alpine roses bloom in meadows that have remained untouched for centuries. Picking them might seem harmless, but many of these species are protected. I've seen tourists pluck edelweiss to press in books, unaware they are breaking Swiss law. Wildlife faces similar risks: ibex, chamois, and marmots may look approachable, but chasing them or feeding them alters their behavior and puts both you and them in danger. I once saw a group scare a herd of chamois near Mürren onto a scree slope—an accident waiting to happen. The Alps are not a petting zoo. Admire nature at a respectful distance and leave it as you found it.

Trespass on Private Land

Swiss landscapes appear open and welcoming, but much of the land is privately owned and used for farming. Trails are made possible because farmers allow them, but stepping beyond marked paths can harm crops or disturb livestock. Once, while hiking near Grindelwald, I saw travelers climb a fence to take a photo with cows—only to be chased back by a protective bull. Trespassing damages the trust that allows Switzerland's extensive trail system to exist. Remember: if a gate is closed, don't open it unless the sign permits passage.

Litter or Ignore Sorting Rules

Switzerland is spotless for a reason: strict waste management. Recycling stations mark bins for PET bottles, glass, and aluminum. Dumping trash in the wrong place, or worse, leaving it on the trail, is both illegal and culturally offensive. I once joined a volunteer clean-up on a ridge above Lake Brienz, collecting dozens of discarded plastic bottles—each one a stain on a pristine view. Always pack out what you bring in, and if you're unsure where to throw something, carry it until you find the correct bin. Locals will respect you more for following their rules of cleanliness.

CHAPTER 9: SHOPPING IN INTERLAKEN

Whenever I return to Interlaken, I never fail to set aside a day simply for wandering its streets with an empty tote bag and a full sense of anticipation. Shopping here is more than acquiring goods; it is a cultural experience where alpine craftsmanship, Swiss precision, and small-town charm blend seamlessly. Between glittering watch displays, the aroma of chocolate shops, and markets that hum with local chatter, Interlaken offers more than souvenirs — it offers pieces of the Alps to take home.

Best Streets and Areas
The heart of shopping in Interlaken lies along Höheweg (46.6866° N, 7.8632° E), the elegant promenade that runs through the center of town. With the snow-draped Jungfrau often visible in the background, this boulevard hosts high-end boutiques, Swiss watch retailers, and luxury

chocolatiers. I have spent countless afternoons here, pausing between shops at sidewalk cafés to people-watch with a cappuccino in hand.

For a more relaxed and authentic feel, I often drift into the streets branching off from Höheweg. Jungfraustrasse and Postgasse are narrower, quieter, and filled with smaller shops where locals buy daily essentials alongside artisan goods. If you cross into Unterseen's historic old town (46.6860° N, 7.8530° E), you'll find cobbled lanes lined with family-run bakeries, woodcarvers, and vintage-style boutiques — a stark contrast to the polished storefronts on Höheweg.

Markets and Boutiques

Markets in Interlaken are lively snapshots of Alpine life. On Saturdays at Interlaken West Railway Square (Bahnhofstrasse 46, 6834 ° N, 7.8505° E), vendors set up stalls offering cheeses from the Bernese Oberland, sausages cured in mountain air, handmade candles, and textiles woven by local families. I still remember chatting with a cheesemaker who explained how his herd grazed at 1,500 meters in summer, lending a distinct herbal note to every bite.

Beyond weekly markets, specialty boutiques abound. Swiss Mountain Market (Höheweg 133) is my go-to for gourmet alpine produce and herbal remedies, while Funky Chocolate Club (Jungfraustrasse 35) offers both irresistible truffles and the chance to craft your own chocolate bars. Step into Heimatwerk (Postgasse 5) and you'll encounter hand-carved cowbells, embroidered fabrics, and toys crafted from natural wood — timeless pieces that tell stories of Swiss tradition.

Swiss-Made Gifts and Souvenirs

Interlaken's shops remind you that Switzerland excels at blending utility with beauty. Watches remain the most prestigious purchase, and boutiques like Bucherer (Höheweg 45) showcase a wide range of brands, from Rolex to Tissot. Each time I enter, I marvel at the precision and artistry behind these timepieces — a reflection of Switzerland's reputation for craftsmanship.

For something edible and universally loved, Swiss chocolate never fails to disappoint. Läderach (Höheweg 115) is famed for its fresh slabs of chocolate studded with nuts and fruits, while Confiserie Schuh (Höheweg 56) adds an artisanal flair to pralines. Sweet enthusiasts should also make a pilgrimage to Meiringen (46.7271° N, 8.1871° E), half an hour away, the birthplace of meringues. Paired with cream from the nearby Alps, it is as indulgent as it is historic.

Other quintessential gifts include wood-carved figurines from Brienz (46.7544° N, 8.0372° E), handwoven woolen goods from Oberland artisans, and, of course, the iconic Swiss Army Knife, available at Victorinox outlets. Each item carries a fragment of Alpine life with it.

Tips and Tax-Free Shopping

Shopping in Switzerland can be a costly affair, but Interlaken provides several ways to maximize value. Always ask for a "Tax-Free" form when spending over CHF 300 in a single shop. With this document, non-EU visitors can claim back up to 7.7% VAT at airports or border points. I make it a point to keep all receipts in a dedicated folder, which simplifies the process.

Shops in Interlaken typically open from 9:00 a.m. to 6:30 p.m. on weekdays, with shorter hours on Saturdays and nearly all closed on Sundays. Credit cards are widely accepted, though smaller boutiques may prefer cash in Swiss francs (CHF). Carrying some change is useful, especially for markets or local bakeries.

Finally, remember etiquette: greet shopkeepers with a polite "Grüezi," avoid haggling (it is not customary in Switzerland), and handle artisan goods with care. Respect earns goodwill, and sometimes even an extra story about the maker behind the product.

Conclusion

Shopping in Interlaken is not just a practical pursuit but a window into Alpine culture. Each street, market stall, and boutique reflects the identity of this mountain town: precise yet warm, traditional yet welcoming to the world. Whether you leave with a luxury watch, a slab of fresh chocolate, or a hand-carved memento, you carry away more than a purchase — you carry a piece of the Bernese Oberland itself.

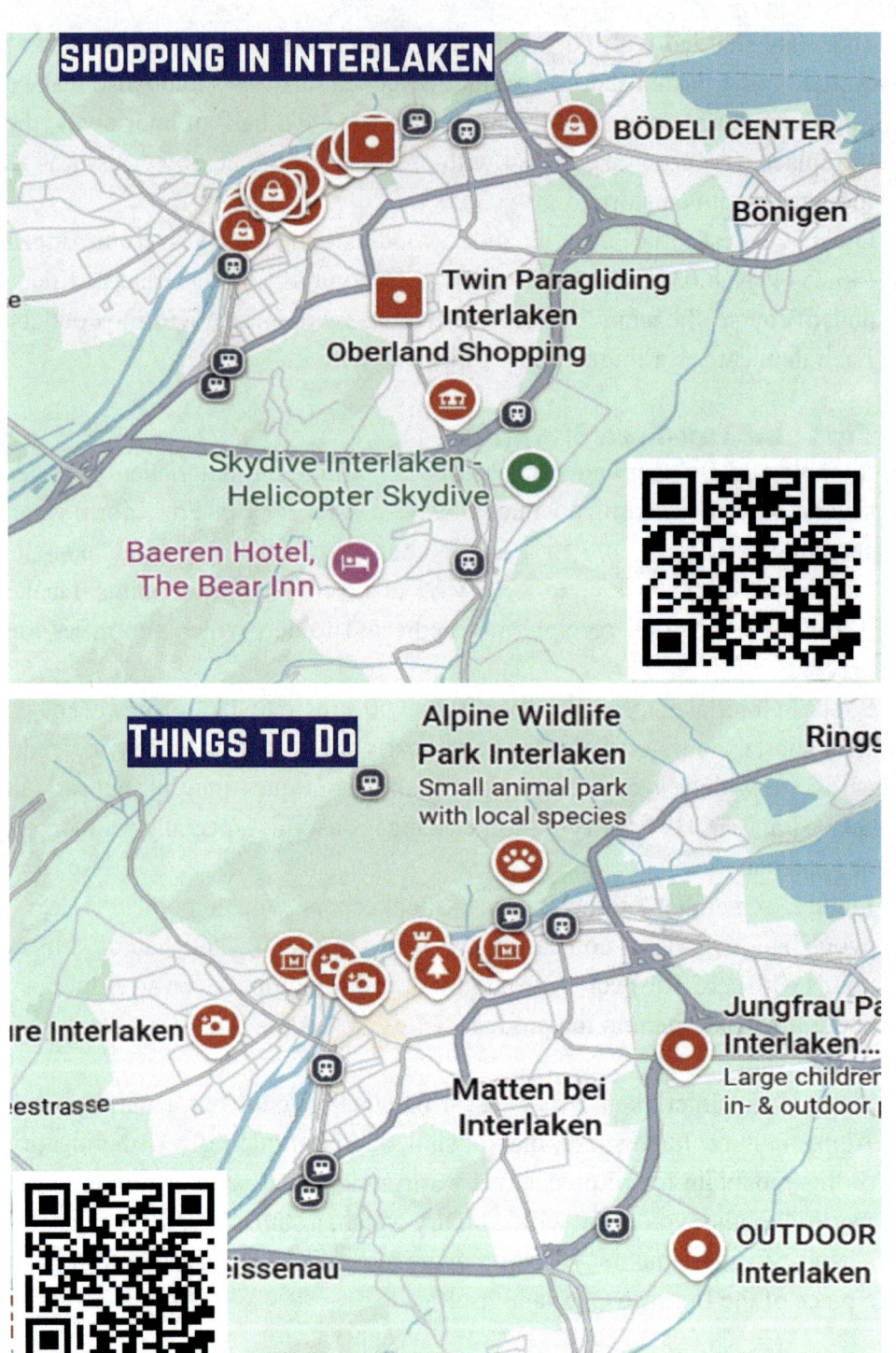

CHAPTER 10: RESPONSIBLE AND SUSTAINABLE TRAVEL

Whenever I set foot in Interlaken, I am reminded that the Swiss Alps are both breathtaking and fragile. The glaciers above Jungfrau feed streams that tumble into waterfalls, the forests provide shelter for deer and ibex, and the lakes shimmer with shades of turquoise found nowhere else. Yet behind the beauty lies a responsibility. These landscapes survive because locals and visitors alike agree to protect them. Responsible travel here is not just encouraged—it is part of the unspoken contract you make when you step into this alpine world.

Low-Impact Travel Tips

On my earliest hikes near Schynige Platte, I learned a lesson I never forgot: the alpine meadows may look robust, but they are among the most delicate ecosystems in Europe. A single misplaced foot can crush wildflowers that take years to recover. That is why I now follow trail markings religiously.

Red-and-white waymarks, painted on rocks and posts, are not decorative—they exist to protect both hikers and the environment.

I also travel light, carrying reusable essentials: a bottle, a fabric shopping bag, and a small container for snacks. In huts such as Berghaus Männdlenen (46.6141° N, 7.9567° E), refilling water is not only welcomed but encouraged. On several hikes above Lauterbrunnen, I watched groups leaving plastic cups behind at picnic sites. The sight was jarring in a country where "leave no trace" is nearly a sacred principle. I now pack an extra bag to carry waste down if I see it.

Wildlife deserves equal respect. I once encountered marmots whistling along the slopes near First. The temptation was to move closer for a better photo, but keeping distance allowed me to observe their natural behavior undisturbed. In Switzerland, feeding or harassing animals is not only disrespectful—it is a fineable offense.

Public Transport and Passes

Few regions in the world make it easier to travel sustainably than the Bernese Oberland. The railways, boats, and lifts connect seamlessly, and using them reduces traffic in valleys that were never designed for cars. From Interlaken Ost Station (46.6911° N, 7.8686° E), I often take the train to Grindelwald in 35 minutes or Lauterbrunnen in 20 minutes. Each ride becomes part of the experience, offering views of rivers and peaks that no highway can rival.

Passes simplify everything. The Swiss Travel Pass grants unlimited travel across trains, boats, and buses throughout the country, while the Jungfrau Travel Pass covers mountain routes up to Jungfraujoch. I once calculated that my three-day Jungfrau Pass saved me nearly CHF 120 compared to buying individual tickets. The Regional Pass Berner Oberland, available at both Interlaken stations, combines flexibility with value.

Using public transport is more than practical—it is cultural. On Lake Thun ferries, I've shared benches with locals commuting between villages, their shopping bags at their feet. On the rack-railway to Schynige Platte, I once sat beside a farmer transporting supplies to his alpine hut. These encounters serve as reminders that trains and boats are lifelines here, not mere tourist novelties.

Water Fountains and Waste Sorting

Switzerland's fountains are small gifts that every traveler should embrace. In Interlaken alone, fountains bubble in Höhematte Park (46.6866° N, 7.8570° E), outside churches, and beside town squares. I carry a stainless-steel bottle and refill it daily with cold alpine water. Locals trust it, and so do I.

Waste sorting is a national ritual. At Coop Interlaken West, the recycling station includes bins for PET, glass (sorted by color), aluminum, and batteries. Compostable waste is collected separately. At first, I found it intimidating—different rules for each material—but the system soon became second nature.

I once misplaced a bottle in the wrong bin, and a passerby politely corrected me. Far from being annoyed, I felt grateful. In Switzerland, sorting waste is not a chore; it is an act of civic pride. By following the system, you not only avoid fines but also show respect for the community you are visiting.

Local Conservation and Alpine Codes

Travelers often overlook the small print at trailheads, yet the Alpine Code of Conduct is a key to traveling responsibly. Its principles are simple: stay on marked routes, respect animals, and leave nothing behind. Over time, I have come to see these codes as more than rules—they are a philosophy of coexistence.

Local conservation efforts are visible everywhere. At the Alpine Garden on Schynige Platte (46.6601° N, 7.8914° E), more than 600 species of mountain plants are cultivated and protected. Entrance fees directly support research and preservation. Visiting there, I felt as though I was walking through a living textbook of alpine ecology.

I have also joined volunteer clean-up hikes organized by local clubs. Carrying a sack and collecting discarded wrappers with Swiss families gave me a sense of belonging. It was humbling to see children treat it as a game, laughing as they competed to fill their bags. That spirit of stewardship—

rooted in generations of alpine living—reminds me why the landscapes here remain pristine.

Closing Note

Traveling responsibly in Interlaken is not about denial or inconvenience. It is about gratitude. Choosing the rack-railway over a car, refilling from a fountain instead of buying bottled water, or respecting a farmer's pasture instead of cutting across it—all of these choices deepen the travel experience.

I often think of sustainability here not as an abstract idea but as a chain. Each traveler who respects the Alps adds a link, keeping the chain unbroken for those who will come after us. For me, Interlaken is not only a destination; it is a reminder that travel is most meaningful when it leaves a place better than we found it.

CHAPTER 11: NATURE AND WILDLIFE IN INTERLAKEN

If Interlaken is a gateway to adventure, then its true heart beats in its landscapes, wildlife, and alpine ecosystems. Few regions in Europe capture the same harmony between water, stone, and life. Every time I return, I am reminded that Interlaken is not only a base for excursions but also a living classroom. Here, nature speaks through glaciers, blossoms, and the calls of animals. Walking these paths means entering a dialogue with the Alps themselves—a reminder that we are visitors in a far older, wilder world.

Landscapes and Lakes

Interlaken lies cradled between Lake Thun to the west and Lake Brienz to the east. These lakes, carved by retreating glaciers, define the geography of the town and give Interlaken its name—"between lakes." On quiet mornings, I often begin with a stroll along the Höhematte Park (46.6869°

N, 7.8553° E). The turquoise glow of Lake Brienz filters through the mist, and the water's clarity comes from glacial melt. Its mineral-rich currents refract shades of emerald and jade that shift with the light.

Lake Thun, broader and deeper, reflects castles and vineyards along its shores. Walking the Thunersee Panoramaweg trail gives wide views of the Bernese Alps mirrored in its waters. By contrast, Lake Brienz feels more intimate, its rugged northern cliffs plunging steeply into the water. A cruise across its surface at sunset, when the sky turns a vibrant violet and gold, offers some of the most breathtaking scenes I have witnessed in Switzerland.

Together, these lakes create microclimates that soften the valleys, allowing fruit orchards to flourish and supporting a surprising variety of plants and birds. They are the lungs and lifeblood of Interlaken's landscape.

Ibex, Chamois, Marmots, and Birds

Hiking in the Bernese Oberland is never just about reaching the summit. It is about who—or what—you meet along the way. Above Schynige Platte (46.6598° N, 7.8792° E), I recall my first sighting of an Alpine ibex (Capra ibex). Their curved horns, etched with age, make them look as though they have stepped out of a medieval tapestry. Once hunted nearly to extinction, the ibex have become symbols of survival, thanks to careful conservation efforts.

Chamois are shyer, darting between crags with a dancer's agility. In early mornings, when the mist still clings to ridges, I have spotted them silhouetted against the rising sun near Niederhorn (46.7137° N, 7.7808° E). Marmots, by contrast, add humor to alpine walks. Their shrill whistles echo across meadows, warning their families of hikers' approach. Sitting quietly near First and Bachalpsee (46.6596° N, 8.0453° E), I once watched a marmot nibble clover, utterly unbothered by my presence.

Birdlife here is equally rich. Golden eagles wheel high above valleys, while nutcrackers and alpine accentors flit through the treeline. Birdwatchers should bring binoculars to Lauterbrunnen Valley (46.5933° N, 7.9091° E), where cliffs and forest edges attract both resident and migratory species. Observing wildlife here is a lesson in patience, humility, and respect.

Alpine Flora and Gardens

The Alps bloom in cycles, each season unveiling a different palette. In early summer, meadows blush with purple gentians, yellow buttercups, and the rare white stars of edelweiss (Leontopodium alpinum)—a flower woven into Swiss identity. I remember kneeling on a ridge above Mürren, holding a delicate edelweiss in my palm, knowing it was both fragile and resilient, surviving only in the harshest conditions.

For travelers wishing to experience this diversity without strenuous climbs, the Alpine Garden at Schynige Platte (46.6598° N, 7.8792° E) is indispensable. Founded in 1927, the garden cultivates over 600 species native to the Swiss Alps, carefully labeled for study. Walking its trails feels like opening a botanic encyclopedia written in petals and stems.

Alpine roses (Rhododendron ferrugineum) add splashes of crimson along slopes in June and July. Their scent mingles with that of pine forests, creating an intoxicating perfume. Every hike becomes a multisensory journey—flowers underfoot, birdsong overhead, and snow peaks framing the horizon.

Protected Areas and Trails

Nature in Interlaken is not accidental—it is safeguarded through strict conservation, ensuring that local ecosystems and species are protected for the future. The Jungfrau-Aletsch UNESCO World Heritage Site (46.5619° N, 8.0361° E) encompasses glaciers, peaks, and valleys, recognized as a landscape of global importance. Hiking trails here are clearly marked, not only to guide visitors but to prevent damage to fragile ecosystems, highlighting the region's ongoing commitment to conservation.

The Schynige Platte–Faulhorn–First trail, for instance, winds across alpine ridges with sweeping panoramas of the Eiger, Mönch, and Jungfrau. Staying on the marked path is essential, both for personal safety and for protecting delicate vegetation. Rangers and local guides often remind travelers that even a single misplaced step can damage plants that take decades to recover.

Local codes emphasize a "leave no trace" ethic: pack out all waste, respect pasture gates, and refrain from making loud noises that disturb wildlife. In many valleys, drone use is restricted, both for safety and to preserve the serenity of the mountains.

Visiting Interlaken is therefore not just about seeing—it is about participating in a culture of stewardship. By following conservation guidelines, each traveler plays a direct role in protecting the landscape and wildlife. This helps ensure that ibex, marmots, and alpine blooms remain for generations to come, making preservation a shared responsibility.

Closing Reflection

As I leave Interlaken's valleys, I always carry with me more than photographs. I carry the memory of a marmot's whistle, the glint of sunlight on Lake Brienz, the quiet dignity of ibex against the snow, and the softness of alpine roses brushing my knees. Knowing Interlaken's nature brings both humility and a sense of uplift. While our footprints may fade, the mountains endure. The responsibility lies with us: tread lightly, listen deeply, and let the Alps speak.

CHAPTER 12: LOCAL ART AND CULTURAL EXPERIENCES

Interlaken is more than just a base for Alpine adventures. It is also a cultural hub where centuries-old traditions meet modern creativity. The town's true charm lies beyond its famous peaks and lakes — in the music halls where alphorns echo, the artisan workshops in Brienz, and the museums where the history of the Bernese Oberland unfolds in vivid detail. This chapter invites readers to explore Interlaken's artistic soul and cultural heartbeat, revealing experiences often missed by travelers rushing to the next mountain summit.

Museums and Galleries

For travelers who enjoy history and art, Interlaken offers a collection of intimate museums and curated galleries that unveil the region's heritage.

- **Tourist Museum of the Jungfrau Region**
  Address: Obere Gasse 28, 3800 Unterseen

Coordinates: 46.6847° N, 7.8510° E

This small yet fascinating museum captures everyday Alpine life from the 19th and early 20th centuries. From traditional farming tools and woodcarving instruments to vintage travel posters and costumes, the exhibits tell the story of Interlaken's evolution into a global tourism center.

- **Kunsthaus Interlaken**
  Address: Jungfraustrasse 55, 3800 Interlaken
  Coordinates: 46.6861° N, 7.8634° E
  Kunsthaus Interlaken is a must-visit for contemporary art lovers. The gallery rotates exhibits featuring Swiss and international artists, showcasing paintings, photography, sculpture, and multimedia art. It is helpful to check their schedule ahead of time, as workshops and live performances are often included.

- **Brienz Rothorn Railway Museum**
  Address: Hauptstrasse 236, 3855 Brienz
  Coordinates: 46.7552° N, 8.0365° E
  For history buffs, this museum celebrates the steam-powered Brienz Rothorn Railway, one of Switzerland's most iconic mountain railways. You can view original steam engines, vintage tickets, and archival photos documenting over a century of Alpine rail history.

These museums are compact and easy to explore in half a day, making them ideal for rainy afternoons or when you want a break from hiking.

Music, Alphorns, and Folk Traditions

Interlaken's cultural identity is deeply tied to Alpine music, where echoes of alphorns, yodels, and folk songs carry across valleys. Attending performances can leave lasting memories for visitors.

- **Swiss Folk Music Evenings**
  At restaurants like Restaurant Laterne (Postgasse 45, 3800 Interlaken; 46.6845° N, 7.8579° E), visitors can enjoy live alphorn demonstrations alongside hearty Swiss dishes. Performances often feature yodeling, accordion melodies, and traditional dances, all performed in colorful Bernese Oberland costumes.

- **Alphorn Festivals**
  One highlight of summer is the annual Alphorn Festival at the Kleine Scheidegg (46.5852° N, 7.9624° E), where dozens of players gather to fill the mountain air with resonant tones. Standing there, surrounded by peaks and sound, is unforgettable.

- **Folk Traditions in Grindelwald and Lauterbrunnen**
  Smaller valleys, such as Lauterbrunnen, host intimate folk evenings where villagers perform local songs passed down through generations. These gatherings offer a unique opportunity to meet locals and gain insight into their connection to the land.

Fairs, Markets, and Seasonal Events

Interlaken's event calendar reflects its dynamic blend of alpine heritage and modern tourism, offering a range of experiences that vary with the seasons.

- **Interlaken Unspunnen Festival**
  Held every 12 years in Interlaken (the next event is expected in 2029), this grand celebration revives traditional Swiss sports, including stone-throwing, wrestling, and flag-spinning, alongside alphorn concerts and folk parades.

- **Brienz Woodcarving Fair**
  Address: Hauptstrasse, 3855 Brienz
  Held every summer, this event transforms the lakeside town into an open-air gallery. Artisans showcase elaborate sculptures, furniture, and carvings, keeping Brienz's centuries-old reputation as the "woodcarving capital of Switzerland" alive.

- **Christmas Markets**
  Between late November and Christmas Eve, Interlaken's Weihnachtsmarkt (Marktplatz, 3800 Interlaken; 46.6848° N, 7.8587° E) lights up with festive stalls. Hot mulled wine, handmade ornaments, and Alpine sweets make this a warm and cozy winter experience.

- **Greenfield Festival**
  For modern music lovers, this open-air festival in June combines

international rock and indie bands with spectacular mountain backdrops at Interlaken Airport.

Travel tip: For the most authentic cultural experiences, check the Jungfrau Region's events calendar before your trip. Plan your visit around village fairs, markets, or festivals that may coincide with hiking or skiing, as dates vary each year. Confirm exact event times and locations with local tourism offices or official event websites to avoid missing out.

Craft Workshops and Woodcarving in Brienz

If you've ever dreamed of taking home a piece of the Alps, Brienz is the place to start. Known as Switzerland's woodcarving heart, this lakeside village has been producing world-class crafts for over 200 years.

- **Schweizer Holzbildhauerschule Brienz (Swiss School of Woodcarving)**
  Address: Hauptstrasse 133, 3855 Brienz
  Coordinates: 46.7547° N, 8.0376° E
  Visitors can observe students and master artisans at work, crafting everything from intricate figurines to full-sized furniture. Short workshops are available for beginners, allowing you to carve your own wooden souvenir under the guidance of professionals.

- **Huggler Woodcarving Studio**
  Address: Hauptstrasse 111, 3855 Brienz
  This historic workshop, which has been operating since 1900, is renowned for producing hand-carved nativity sets and custom sculptures. Guided tours provide insight into how traditional techniques are combined with modern tools.
- **Shopping Tip**: Look for the "Brienz Certification Mark" on woodcarvings to ensure you are buying local, high-quality, and authentic pieces directly from Brienz artisans.

CHAPTER 13: HIDDEN BEACHES AND SECRET SPOTS

When most travelers picture Interlaken, they see snow-capped peaks, turquoise lakes, and bustling adventure hubs. But the true soul of this region lies in its quiet corners — hidden lakeshores, secret sunset ridges, and secluded alpine valleys where the locals retreat. Over years of exploring every trail and inlet, I've uncovered places most visitors never find. This chapter presents my curated list of Interlaken's best-kept secrets, ideal for those seeking solitude, natural beauty, and authentic Swiss charm.

Quiet Lakeshores and Piers

Neuhaus Beach — Lake Thun's Secret Escape
- **Address:** Neuhausstrasse 45, 3800 Unterseen
- **Coordinates:** 46.6748° N, 7.7949° E

One of my favorite hideaways, Neuhaus Beach, is just 3 km from central Interlaken. Unlike Höheweg's busy waterfront, Neuhaus remains serene even in peak season. Its soft pebble beach, shallow turquoise waters, and shaded pine groves make it ideal for quiet picnics.

What to Do:
- Rent a kayak from Neuhaus Watersports (from CHF 20/hour).
- Dine at the Neuhaus Golf & Strandhotel Restaurant, where lake fish is always fresh.
- Stay for the golden hour — the views of Niesen Peak glowing under the setting sun are unforgettable.

Bönigen's Hidden Lido — Family-Friendly Bliss
- **Address:** Lütschinenstrasse, 3806 Bönigen
- **Coordinates:** 46.6873° N, 7.9012° E

This is where locals gather when they want calm waters without the crowds. A small grassy park meets Lake Brienz's glassy shoreline, perfect for families. Amenities include playgrounds, BBQ spots, and shallow swimming areas.

Insider Tip: Visit at sunrise when the peaks reflect perfectly on the lake's surface — an unforgettable photo opportunity.

Ringgenberg Pier — A Photographer's Secret
- **Address:** Strandbad Ringgenberg, 3852 Ringgenberg
- **Coordinates:** 46.7155° N, 7.8921° E

This tiny wooden pier stretches into the turquoise waters of Lake Brienz and offers picture-perfect compositions without the tourist rush.

Secret Viewpoints and Sunset Ridges

Harder Kulm Hidden Path
Most people crowd the viewing platform at Harder Kulm, but a short, unmarked trail behind the restaurant leads to a quieter rock ledge with panoramic views of two lakes.

Best Time: Sunset in late June when alpine peaks glow in pastel hues.
Bring: A lightweight jacket — temperatures drop fast even in summer.

Augstmatthorn Ridge — Wildlife Meets Wilderness
- **Coordinates:** 46.7543° N, 7.9001° E

This ridge hike rewards you with sweeping alpine panoramas and an almost guaranteed chance to spot wild ibex herds at dawn. It's a moderate 4-hour trek from Lombachalp, but the solitude is worth every step.

Off-the-Beaten-Path Villages and Valleys

Iseltwald — The Fairytale Village
- **Address:** Dorfstrasse, 3807 Iseltwald
- **Coordinates:** 46.7164° N, 7.9671° E

With its wooden chalets, flower-decked balconies, and lakeside pier, Iseltwald feels like a scene from a Swiss postcard. The historic Seeburg Castle adds a romantic backdrop, especially at dusk.

Saxeten Valley — A World Away
- **Coordinates:** 46.6412° N, 7.8737° E

Hidden between towering cliffs, Saxeten offers untouched alpine meadows, rushing waterfalls, and complete silence. It's also a great starting point for guided canyoning adventures.
Getting There: Regular buses depart from Interlaken West (**approximately** 20 minutes).

Giessbach Falls and Historic Grandhotel
- **Address:** Axalpstrasse, 3855 Brienz
- **Coordinates:** 46.7390° N, 8.0331° E

Accessible by vintage funicular, these 14-tiered waterfalls are one of Lake Brienz's most breathtaking sights. Stay for lunch at the Grandhotel Giessbach, an architectural masterpiece dating back to 1875.

Summary Insight: Interlaken's hidden gems aren't always on the map — they're found in quiet sunrises, forgotten trails, and alpine villages where life slows down.

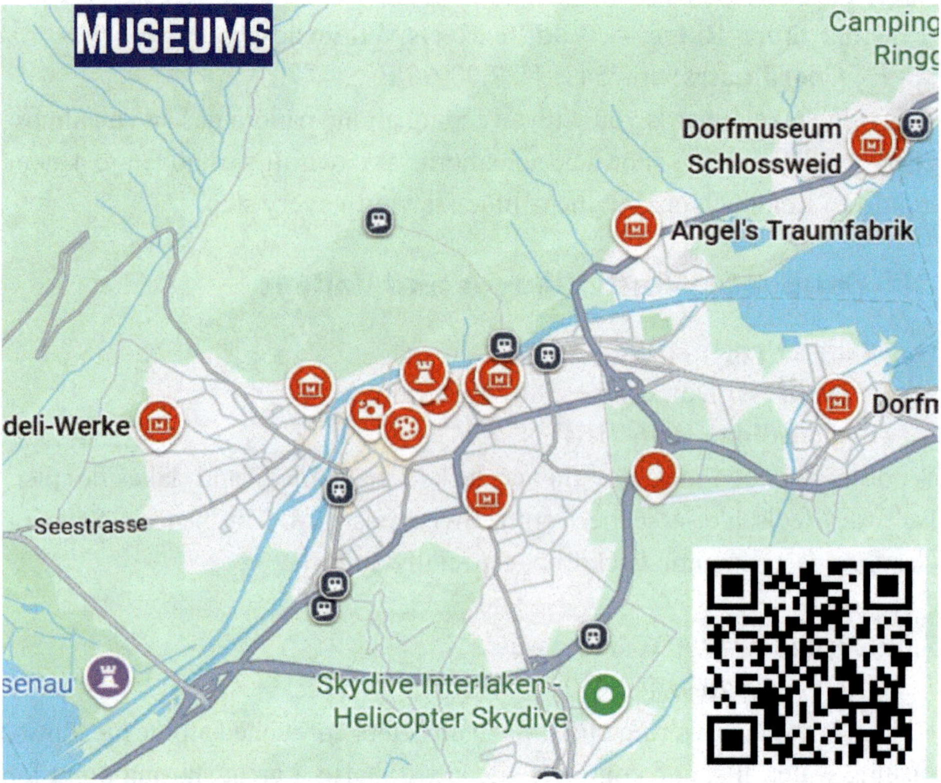
MUSEUMS
Camping
Ringg
Dorfmuseum
Schlossweid
Angel's Traumfabrik
deli-Werke
Dorfn
Seestrasse
senau
Skydive Interlaken -
Helicopter Skydive

Bern
5
6
2
2
2
10
1
3
4
7
8
9
Reichenbach
Falls
Eiger, Mönch
and Jungfrau

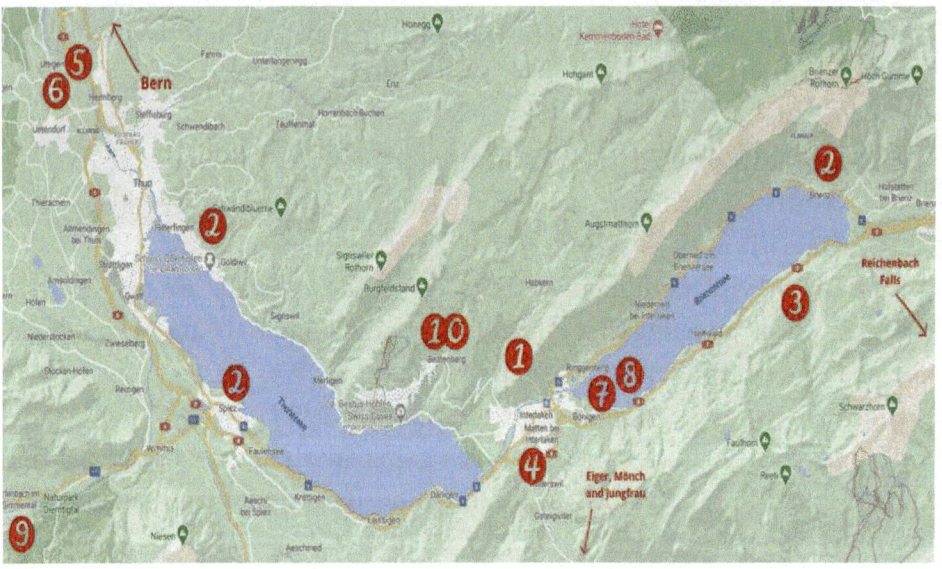

CHAPTER 14: TIPS FOR TRAVELING WITH KIDS

Traveling through Interlaken with children can be magical if you plan wisely. Over the years, I've explored the region with families, and I've learned that the key to a successful trip lies in balancing outdoor adventure, interactive learning, and relaxing downtime. Interlaken is uniquely suited for this, with safe walking paths, child-friendly attractions, playful lakeshores, and engaging cultural experiences that allow both adults and kids to enjoy themselves fully.

This chapter provides a comprehensive guide to family-focused travel in the region — from gentle walks and picnic stops to interactive museums, kid-approved restaurants, and water-based activities. I've also included tips on transport passes, safety, and seasonal recommendations to make your trip seamless.

Family-Friendly Walks and Playgrounds

Aare River Promenade — Gentle Walk with Stroller Access
- **Address:** Aarmühlestrasse, 3800 Interlaken
- **Coordinates:** 46.6867° N, 7.8604° E

Whenever I visit Interlaken with families, the Aare River Promenade is my first recommendation. This flat, shaded walking path connects Interlaken West and Ost, offering peaceful riverside views without heavy crowds.

Why Kids Love It:
- Ducks and swans often gather along the riverbanks.
- Plenty of benches for snack breaks.
- Wide paths perfect for strollers and bikes.

Tip: Stop at Hohematte Park along the way. It has a large grassy field where children can run freely while parents enjoy the views of Jungfrau Peak.

Alpenwildpark Interlaken — Free Animal Park
- **Address:** Harderstrasse 35, 3800 Interlaken
- **Coordinates:** 46.6911° N, 7.8640° E

This small wildlife park near Harder Kulm Station is a hidden favorite for local families. Kids can watch marmots and ibex up close without any entrance fees.

Best Time to Visit: Early morning feedings when animals are most active.

Spielplatz Höhematte — Interlaken's Central Playground
- **Address:** Höheweg 105, 3800 Interlaken
- **Coordinates:** 46.6864° N, 7.8617° E

Set within the town's largest open park, this playground has slides, swings, and climbing nets, all with panoramic mountain views. Parents can sit back at nearby cafés while kids play safely.

Child-Friendly Restaurants and Cafés
OX Restaurant & Grill
- **Address:** Höheweg 1, 3800 Interlaken
- **Coordinates:** 46.6859° N, 7.8572° E

One of my top dining picks for families, OX offers kid-sized portions, coloring kits, and a relaxed atmosphere. Their Swiss-style macaroni and cheese (Älplermagronen) is always a hit.

Restaurant Neuhaus am See
- **Address:** Neuhausstrasse 45, 3800 Unterseen
- **Coordinates:** 46.6748° N, 7.7949° E

Located right on Lake Thun's shoreline, this restaurant combines fresh air, beautiful scenery, and kid-friendly menus. Families often pair a meal here with boat rentals or paddleboard sessions nearby.

Backerei Mohler *(Local Favorite)*
- **Address:** Jungfraustrasse 35, 3800 Interlaken
- **Coordinates:** 46.6869° N, 7.8614° E

For quick, budget-friendly lunches, Mohler is perfect. Their fresh pastries, sandwiches, and hot chocolates keep kids happy between excursions.

Interactive Museums and Learning Stops
JungfrauPark Interlaken — Science Meets Fun
- **Address:** Obere Bönigstrasse 100, 3800 Interlaken
- **Coordinates:** 46.6815° N, 7.8810° E

This family-oriented science park blends entertainment and education. Kids can explore interactive exhibits on natural wonders, space, and alpine geology.

Tip: Book tickets online to avoid queues — family passes are available for CHF 65.

Ballenberg Open-Air Museum
- **Address:** Museumsstrasse 100, 3858 Hofstetten
- **Coordinates:** 46.7483° N, 8.0374° E

This open-air museum is one of Switzerland's best learning experiences for kids. Set on 66 hectares, Ballenberg features historic Swiss houses, craft workshops, and farm animals. Children can watch cheesemakers at work, learn woodcarving, or join hands-on bread-baking sessions.

Tourismuseum Unterseen
- **Address:** Obere Gasse 28, 3800 Unterseen
- **Coordinates:** 46.6841° N, 7.8504° E

This small museum showcases vintage sleds, alpine gear, and mountaineering history — great for sparking curiosity in young adventurers.

Best Pools, Lidos, and Lake Beaches
Bönigen Lido *(Family Top Pick)*
- **Address:** Lütschinenstrasse, 3806 Bönigen
- **Coordinates:** 46.6873° N, 7.9012° E

With shallow waters, sandy edges, and plenty of shade, Bönigen Lido is my go-to recommendation for families with toddlers and young kids. Lifeguards are on duty in summer.

Neuhaus Beach — Water Sports Hub
I also recommend Neuhaus for families who enjoy more **active water fun**, including paddleboarding, kayaking, and renting pedal boats.

Burgseeli Natural Pool
- **Address:** Seestrasse 100, 3800 Goldswil
- **Coordinates:** 46.7007° N, 7.8769° E

This warm, shallow natural pool sits hidden among pine forests and is perfect for kids learning to swim. There's a small café and playground onsite.

Summary Insight:
Interlaken makes traveling with kids effortless. Between gentle walks, interactive museums, and family-friendly dining, there's plenty to fill your days without overstretching young travelers.

CHAPTER 15: INTERLAKEN'S NIGHTLIFE AND AFTER-HOURS SCENE

When the sun sets behind the Jungfrau massif and the alpine peaks fade into shades of purple and gold, Interlaken reveals a different side of itself. While the region is widely known for its outdoor adventures and daytime scenery, the evenings are just as captivating, offering intimate bars, riverside lounges, sunset cruises, and cultural experiences that bring the town alive after dark.

Over the years, I've wandered Interlaken's streets, explored its hidden nightlife corners, and found spots perfect for every mood — whether you want lively music, quiet lakefront evenings, or sophisticated dining under the stars. This chapter is your curated guide to the best of Interlaken after hours.

Top Bars and Lounges

Hüsi Bierhaus — For Local Swiss Brews
- **Address:** Postgasse 3, 3800 Interlaken
- **Coordinates:** 46.6849° N, 7.8547° E

Hüsi Bierhaus is Interlaken's craft beer haven, with over 20 taps featuring both Swiss and international brews. The rustic wooden interiors create a cozy alpine vibe, and the staff are always ready to recommend pairings with their signature cheese platters.
Insider Tip: Arrive before 8 PM to avoid queues. Fridays often feature live folk music nights — highly recommended for a taste of Swiss culture.

Oberland Bar — Classic Alpine Cocktail Spot
- **Address:** Höheweg 7, 3800 Interlaken
- **Coordinates:** 46.6868° N, 7.8610° E

Set in a stylish lounge overlooking the Höhematte Park, Oberland Bar is my go-to for signature cocktails. The bartenders are inventive, using local alpine herbs in their mixes.
Best For: Couples and small groups seeking a relaxed evening atmosphere with occasional piano sessions.

Balmer's Metro Bar — Youthful and Energetic
- **Address:** Hauptstrasse 23, 3800 Matten bei Interlaken
- **Coordinates:** 46.6789° N, 7.8632° E

Located inside the historic Balmer's Hostel, this is the epicenter of Interlaken's backpacker nightlife. Expect DJ nights, neon lights, and themed parties during the summer. Drinks are affordable, and the crowd is diverse and lively.

Riverside Lounge — Chic and Scenic
- **Address:** Aarestrasse 38, 3800 Interlaken
- **Coordinates:** 46.6843° N, 7.8602° E

If you prefer a calmer riverside evening, Riverside Lounge offers elegant outdoor seating right beside the Aare River. It's perfect for wine lovers — the curated Swiss wine list is one of the best in town.

Live Music Venues

Johnny's Pub — Rock and Acoustic Nights
- **Address:** Marktgasse 22, 3800 Unterseen
- **Coordinates:** 46.6841° N, 7.8529° E

Johnny's is a small yet legendary venue known for its open-mic sessions, live rock gigs, and acoustic storytelling evenings. The setting is intimate, making it perfect for music enthusiasts who enjoy close-up performances.

Kreuz & Quer Kulturhaus *(Seasonal Performances)*
- **Address:** Spielmatte 12, 3800 Interlaken
- **Coordinates:** 46.6853° N, 7.8520° E

This cultural hub regularly hosts folk music, world music nights, and local theater productions. It's an excellent choice if you want to dive into Interlaken's artistic and cultural nightlife beyond the typical bar scene.

Hotel Interlaken's Lounge & Live Sessions
- **Address:** Höheweg 74, 3800 Interlaken
- **Coordinates:** 46.6866° N, 7.8623° E

Every Wednesday and Saturday evening, Hotel Interlaken transforms its elegant lounge into a live jazz and classical venue. Their candlelit ambiance, paired with soft tunes, makes this a top pick for couples.

Evening Cruises and Events

Lake Thun Dinner Cruise
- **Departure Point:** Interlaken West Pier
- **Coordinates:** 46.6818° N, 7.8426° E

For a romantic evening, few experiences rival a sunset dinner cruise on Lake Thun. The 2.5-hour journey glides past medieval castles, lakeside villages, and mountain reflections. Expect a multi-course Swiss dinner on deck while local musicians set the mood.

Cost: CHF 79 per adult (dinner included). Booking in advance is essential during summer.

Brienz Lake Lantern Cruise *(Seasonal)*
- **Departure Point:** Interlaken Ost Pier
- **Coordinates:** 46.6913° N, 7.8697° E

This lesser-known option offers lantern-lit boat rides across Lake Brienz on evenings in July and August. The experience is quiet, intimate, and especially magical for families.

Summer Outdoor Cinemas
Every July, Höhematte Park hosts a series of open-air movie nights, complete with food stalls and beanbag seating. Bring a picnic blanket, and you'll enjoy one of the most atmospheric evenings in Interlaken.

Late-Night Dining

Restaurant Laterne
- **Address:** Jungfraustrasse 37, 3800 Interlaken
- **Coordinates:** 46.6873° N, 7.8615° E

Serving until 11:30 PM, Laterne is perfect if your evening stretches late. Their specialties include raclette, fondue, and grilled meats — a must-try for first-time visitors.

Goldener Anker
- **Address:** Marktgasse 57, 3800 Interlaken
- **Coordinates:** 46.6835° N, 7.8517° E

A popular pub-restaurant hybrid with hearty burgers, vegetarian-friendly dishes, and live acoustic sets in the evenings.

Snack Bistro Interlaken *(Budget-Friendly)*
- **Address:** Untere Bönigstrasse 8, 3800 Interlaken
- **Coordinates:** 46.6855° N, 7.8661° E

For those late-night cravings after 10 PM, this small eatery offers fresh sandwiches, wraps, and Swiss hotdogs — ideal after an evening out.

CHAPTER 16: BEST LUXURY EXPERIENCES IN INTERLAKEN

Interlaken is often referred to as the "gateway to the Bernese Oberland," but for luxury travelers, it is much more than just a base for exploring the Alps. Over the years, I've experienced Interlaken at its finest—staying in grand suites, dining at chef's tables, chartering private helicopters, and unwinding in destination spas surrounded by snow-dusted peaks. Here, luxury blends with nature: turquoise lakes reflect the Jungfrau massif, while refined Swiss hospitality curates every moment. Whether you dream of sipping champagne on a private yacht, indulging in a spa retreat, or tasting gourmet dishes above the clouds, Interlaken delivers exclusive experiences that redefine alpine luxury.

Iconic Grand Hotels and Signature Suites

If Interlaken has a crown jewel, it is the Victoria-Jungfrau Grand Hotel & Spa (Höheweg 41, 3800 Interlaken; 46.6861° N, 7.8561° E). Established in

1865, this Belle Époque landmark embodies elegance with its marble corridors, crystal chandeliers, and sweeping views of the Jungfrau. Suites offer indulgence: panoramic terraces, private living rooms, personal butlers, and exclusive spa access. Rates start near CHF 1,200 per night for junior suites, but the service and exclusivity are unrivaled.

Another historic address is the Lindner Grand Hotel Beau Rivage (Höheweg 211, 3800 Interlaken), set along the emerald Aare River. Its riverside suites feature balconies with views of the Bernese Alps, accompanied by Michelin-rated dining in select packages. For boutique opulence, Hotel Royal St. Georges combines vintage charm with contemporary amenities, making it ideal for those seeking intimacy and luxury.

Insider Tip: Request the Victoria Suite at the Victoria-Jungfrau for breathtaking floor-to-ceiling views of the Jungfrau. Guests enjoy private transfers, bespoke concierge services, and exclusive spa treatments tailored to their individual wellness goals.

Private Guides, Helicopters, and Lake Charters

For travelers seeking extraordinary **experiences**, Interlaken offers private tours blending adventure and exclusivity. The ultimate indulgence is a helicopter flight with Swiss Helicopter AG (Flugplatz Interlaken, 3800 Interlaken; 46.6763° N, 7.8793° E), where a private pilot flies you over the Eiger, Mönch, Jungfrau, and Aletsch Glacier. Packages start at CHF 3,200 for two guests and can include champagne landings on secluded glaciers.

For a different perspective, consider booking a luxury yacht or motorboat on Lake Brienz or Lake Thun. Companies like BLS Navigation offer bespoke itineraries—from sunset champagne cruises to private wine tastings on crewed vessels. Rates start at CHF 1,000 for a two-hour charter, which includes curated Swiss wines and gourmet platters.

Prefer land? Hire a personal guide through Swiss Alpine Guides. Specialists craft tailored itineraries—hidden glacier walks, private photo safaris, and VIP access to exclusive viewpoints normally reserved for locals.

Pro Tip: Book helicopter tours for the early morning to enjoy the clearest alpine skies and optimal photography opportunities.

High-End Dining and Chef's Tables

Interlaken's culinary scene rivals its scenery, offering Michelin-starred and chef-driven menus that celebrate Alpine heritage.

Start at La Terrasse Brasserie at Victoria-Jungfrau Grand Hotel, where French technique meets local Alpine ingredients. Multi-course tasting menus start at CHF 160 per person, accompanied by a curated *selection of* Swiss wines.

For something extraordinary, reserve The Barrel Lounge (Höheweg 37, 3800 Interlaken), where chef's table diners interact with culinary masters. Seasonal tasting menus are paired with sommelier-selected, boutique Swiss vintages.

For dining above the clouds, visit the Schilthorn Piz Gloria revolving restaurant in Mürren, 3825 Lauterbrunnen (46.5574° N, 7.8353° E). At 2,970 meters, enjoy 360° views of the Bernese Alps with veal Zurich-style, truffle risotto, and perch from Lake Thun.

Insider Tip: Book the sunset dinner package at Schilthorn Piz Gloria — timed so the final course arrives as the sun dips behind the Jungfrau massif.

Destination Spas and Wellness Retreats

Interlaken's wellness offerings are transformative. The Victoria-Jungfrau Spa, spanning 5,500 square meters, features hydrotherapy pools, thermal circuits, and alpine botanical treatments for deep relaxation. Signature experiences include aromatic stone massages, anti-aging facials, and salt chambers.

For lakeside tranquility, visit Deltapark Vitalresort (Deltaweg 29, 3645 Gwatt, Thun; 46.7333° N, 7.6339° E). Surrounded by nature reserves, the resort offers detox programs, thermal baths, and spa suites with stunning views of Lake Thun. Tailored wellness packages start around CHF 700 per day, including nutrition consultations.

If mountain serenity is your goal, Beatus Wellness & Spa Hotel, located near St. Beatus Caves, offers infinity pools with stunning lake views, open-air Jacuzzis, and botanical therapies that utilize local alpine herbs.

Insider Tip: Opt for a spa package that combines outdoor yoga, guided mindfulness walks, and nutrition consultations for a comprehensive body reset.

Conclusion

Luxury in Interlaken is defined not by excess, but by thoughtful exclusivity—experiences tailored to the individual, framed by the Swiss Alps. Whether soaring above glaciers, savoring haute cuisine, unwinding in infinity pools, or cruising secluded lakeshores, this alpine sanctuary delivers elevated indulgence.

CHAPTER 17: SOCIAL MEDIA SPOTS AND INSTAGRAM-WORTHY LOCATIONS

When I arrived in Interlaken, I didn't expect to find so many postcard-like spots. I soon realized the region offers more than mountain adventures and serene lakes—it's among Europe's most photogenic places. From landscapes and waterfalls to alpine villages, Interlaken offers endless stunning photo opportunities. Here are my top Instagram-worthy locations, selected through personal exploration and insider tips.

Top Viewpoints and Footbridges

Harder Kulm – The "Top of Interlaken"
Address: Harderbahn Valley Station, Untere Bönigstrasse 5, 3800 Interlaken
Coordinates: 46.7013° N, 7.8660° E

Harder Kulm rises 1,321 meters above sea level and is Interlaken's most famous viewpoint. I remember stepping onto the Two-Lakes Bridge, with Lake Thun on one side, Lake Brienz on the other, and the Jungfrau, Mönch, and Eiger peaks framed in the background. Visit early in the morning for soft light or late in the evening for sunset glows. Take the 10-minute funicular from Interlaken Ost; book ahead in peak season to avoid disappointment.

Sigriswil Panorama Bridge
Address: Dorfstrasse 57, 3655 Sigriswil
Coordinates: 46.7167° N, 7.7222° E
Spanning 340 meters over Gummischlucht Gorge, this suspension bridge offers dramatic views of Lake Thun and the Bernese Alps. It's quieter than Harder Kulm, ideal for uninterrupted shots. Arrive mid-morning when sunlight makes the water pop turquoise against green hillsides.

Mürren Skyline Trail
Coordinates: 46.5586° N, 7.8915° E
Accessible by cable car from Lauterbrunnen, Mürren's Skyline Trail is a photographer's paradise. The path features 360-degree alpine panoramas, rustic huts, and wildflower meadows. Visit in late spring or early summer for snow-capped peaks and vibrant trails.

Waterfalls and Lakeside Piers
After exploring high viewpoints, it's time to discover Interlaken's magnificent waterfalls and tranquil lakeside spots.
Coordinates: 46.7391° N, 8.0334° E
Tucked within a dense forest above Lake Brienz, Giessbach Falls cascades down 14 terraces to turquoise water. A short hike leads behind a waterfall, perfect for dramatic shots. Late afternoon sunlight, filtered through the mist, creates the best photos.

Staubbach Falls

Address: Lauterbrunnen Valley, 3822 Lauterbrunnen
Coordinates: 46.5933° N, 7.9090° E

Staubbach, one of Switzerland's tallest free-falling waterfalls, drops nearly 300 meters down Lauterbrunnen's cliffs. Sunrise paints the mist in gold—an unforgettable view. Add a village walk for alpine street photography.

Lakeside Piers of Brienz and Thun

For minimalist photos, visit the wooden piers on Lake Brienz (Iseltwald: 46.7063° N, 7.9606° E) and Lake Thun (46.7385° N, 7.6236° E). Early mornings offer mirror-like reflections. These are great for drone shots—always check local rules first.

Secret Locations for Sunrise and Sunset

Schynige Platte Ridge
Coordinates: 46.6582° N, 7.9048° E

Schynige Platte is a hidden gem offering panoramic views of the Eiger, Mönch, and Jungfrau, without the crowds of Jungfraujoch. Arrive at dawn to capture mountains glowing pink-orange and wildflowers lit by first light.

Ringgenberg Castle Ruins

Address: Burgstrasse, 3852 Ringgenberg
Coordinates: 46.7158° N, 7.8929° E

Above Lake Brienz, these medieval ruins are among Interlaken's most romantic sunset spots. It's usually quiet and ideal for peaceful landscapes or couple portraits framed by the lake and mountains.

Isenfluh Hidden Viewpoint
Coordinates: 46.5945° N, 7.8904° E

Above Lauterbrunnen, Isenfluh is a tiny hamlet with breathtaking views of cliffs and valleys. Few tourists visit, making it an ideal destination for unique content. Sunsets are magical, with pastel skies reflecting on snowy ridges.

Final Tips for Capturing Interlaken

- Aim for early morning or late evening, the golden hour, to get softer light and fewer crowds in your shots—maximizing photo impact.
- **Choose your season based on desired colors:** spring for wildflowers, summer for greens, autumn for golds, and winter for snowy charm.
- **Bring a** wide-angle lens for landscapes and a lightweight tripod for sharp, low-light images—key gear for Interlaken.
- **Drone Photography**: Always check Swiss airspace restrictions before flying.

CHAPTER 18: LOCAL LANGUAGE AND PHRASES GUIDE

Exploring Interlaken and the surrounding Jungfrau region is more rewarding when you understand the rhythm of its local language. While many people here speak English, a few well-placed phrases in German or Swiss German can transform interactions, earn warm smiles, and open doors to authentic cultural moments. During my travels, I found that even simple greetings made me feel more connected to the community, especially in smaller alpine villages where Swiss German is the everyday norm.

German and Swiss German Basics

Interlaken is situated in the Bernese Oberland region of Switzerland, where both High German (Hochdeutsch) and Swiss German (Schweizerdeutsch) are spoken. High German is the country's official written language, used in menus, official documents, train announcements, and signage. Swiss

German, on the other hand, is a **spoken dialect**, and it varies slightly from canton to canton.

In Interlaken, you'll often hear **Bernese Swiss German**. For example:
- "Good morning" in High German: **Guten Morgen** (pronounced *GOO-ten MOR-gen*)
- In Swiss German, it's **Guete Morge** (pronounced *GWEH-te MOR-ge*).

While you don't need to master Swiss German to navigate Interlaken, learning to recognize its melody helps you follow local conversations. In formal settings, such as hotels or restaurants, Hochdeutsch is always understood. But in villages like Lauterbrunnen or Grindelwald, even a few dialect words—like Grüezi (*hello*) or Merci vielmal (*thank you very much*)—go a long way.

Useful Expressions and Signs

During my visits, I noticed that most public spaces—train stations, cable car terminals, hiking trail markers—are labeled in German first, sometimes accompanied by English or French. Understanding these basic expressions helps travelers navigate confidently.

Common Travel Signs in German:
- **Eingang** – Entrance
- **Ausgang** – Exit
- **Gleis** – Train platform
- **Fahrplan** – Timetable
- **Kasse** – Ticket counter
- **Richtung** – Direction
- **Wanderweg** – Hiking trail
- **Seilbahn** – Cable car

In cafés and mountain huts, here are the phrases I used most:
- **Einen Kaffee, bitte** (*AY-nen KAH-fee, BIT-te*) – "One coffee, please."
- **Noch ein Glas Wasser, bitte** (*NOCH ine GLAHS VAS-ser*) – "Another glass of water, please."

- **Kann ich mit Karte bezahlen?** (*KAHN ish mit KAR-te be-ZAH-len?*) – "Can I pay by card?"

Pro tip: Many menus in Interlaken are multilingual, but knowing the German names for local dishes helps you spot authentic specialties, such as Rösti, Älplermagronen, and Meiringer Meringues.

Common Phrases for Travelers

Whether you're buying train tickets, hiking to a mountain hut, or ordering fondue, these simple phrases make day-to-day interactions smoother:

Greetings and Polite Words:
- **Grüezi!** (*GRUHT-see*) – Hello (common in Bernese Oberland)
- **Hoi!** (*Hoy!*) – Informal hi, used among locals
- **Danke** (*DAHN-ke*) – Thank you
- **Bitte** (*BIT-te*) – Please / You're welcome

Getting Around:
- **Wo ist der Bahnhof?** (*Vo ist der BAHN-hof?*) – "Where is the train station?"
- **Wie viel kostet das Ticket?** (*Vee feel KOH-stet das TIK-ket?*) – "How much is the ticket?"
- **Geht dieser Zug nach Grindelwald?** (*Gate DEE-ser tsoog nahk GRIN-del-vald?*) – "Does this train go to Grindelwald?"

Dining and Shopping:
- **Haben Sie einen Tisch frei?** (*HAH-ben zee AY-nen tish fry?*) – "Do you have a free table?"
- **Ich nehme das Menü** (*Ish NAY-me das MEN-yoo*) – "I'll take the menu."
- **Wie spät haben Sie geöffnet?** (*Vee shpate HAH-ben zee geh-OFF-net?*) – "What time do you open?"

Traveler's Tip

If you want to dive deeper, the Tourist Information Center at Höheweg 37, 3800 Interlaken (GPS: 46.6865° N, 7.8632° E) offers free phrase cards and multilingual brochures. I picked one up on my first trip, and it became my go-to reference for spontaneous conversations.

Essential German & Swiss German Phrases for Travelers
A. Greetings & Everyday Phrases

English	German	Swiss German	Pronunciation
Hello	Guten Tag	Grüezi	GOO-ten Tahg / GRUHT-see
Hi (informal)	Hallo	Hoi	HAH-lo / Hoy
Good morning	Guten Morgen	Guete Morge	GOO-ten MOR-gen / GWEH-te MOR-ge
Good evening	Guten Abend	Guete Abig	GOO-ten AH-bent / GWEH-te AH-big
Goodbye	Auf Wiedersehen	Adieu / Tschüss	OWF VEE-der-zayn / TSHUESS
Please	Bitte	Bitte	BIT-te
Thank you	Danke	Merci / Merci vielmal	DAHN-ke / MER-see feel-mal
Yes	Ja	Ja	Yah
No	Nein	Nei	Nine
Excuse me	Entschuldigung	Exgüsi	Ent-SHOOL-dee-goong / EX-gyoo-see
Do you speak English?	Sprechen Sie Englisch?	Schprechid Si Englisch?	SHPRECH-en zee ENG-lish

B. Getting Around & Transport

English	German	Swiss German	Pronunciation
Where is the train station?	Wo ist der Bahnhof?	Wo isch de Bahnhof?	Vo ist der BAHN-hof / Vo ish de BAHN-hof
Which platform?	Welches Gleis?	Wälches Gleis?	VEL-hes GLICE
How much is the ticket?	Wie viel kostet das Ticket?	Wie viel koschtet s Billett?	Vee feel KOH-stet das TIK-ket

English	German	Swiss German	Pronunciation
Does this train go to Grindelwald?	Fährt dieser Zug nach Grindelwald?	Fährt dä Zug nach Grindelwald?	Faert DEE-ser tsoog nahk GRIN-del-vald
When is the next bus?	Wann fährt der nächste Bus?	Wänn fahrt dä nöchste Bus?	Vahn faert der NEX-teh boos
Ticket counter	Fahrkartenschalter	Billettschalter	FAR-kar-ten-shal-ter

C. Dining & Ordering Food

English	German	Swiss German	Pronunciation
A table for two, please	Einen Tisch für zwei, bitte	Es Tischli für zwei, bitte	AY-nen TISH füer TSVY, BIT-te
I'll take this dish	Ich nehme dieses Gericht	Ich näh das Gericht	Ish NAY-me DEE-ses ge-RIKHT
The menu, please	Die Speisekarte, bitte	d'Speiskarte, bitte	DEE SHPY-ze-KAR-teh BIT-te
Water	Wasser	Wasser	VAH-ser
Beer	Bier	Bier	BEER
Coffee	Kaffee	Kafi	KAH-feh / KAH-fee
The bill, please	Die Rechnung, bitte	D'Rächnig, bitte	DEE RECH-noong / DEH-RECH-nig

D. Shopping & Payments

English	German	Swiss German	Pronunciation
How much does this cost?	Wie viel kostet das?	Wievil koschtet das?	Vee feel KOH-stet das
Do you accept cards?	Nehmen Sie Karten?	Nähmed Si Chärtli?	NAY-men zee KAR-ten
Where is the cashier?	Wo ist die Kasse?	Wo isch d'Chasse?	Vo ist dee KAH-seh
Can I get a receipt?	Kann ich eine Quittung bekommen?	Chani e Quittig ha?	KAH-nee eye-ne KVIT-toong

E. Hiking & Outdoor Adventures

English	German	Swiss German	Pronunciation
Hiking trail	Wanderweg	Wanderwäg	VAN-der-VEYG
Cable car	Seilbahn	Seilbähn	ZYLE-bahn
Is the trail open?	Ist der Weg offen?	Isch dä Wäg offe?	Ist der VEGH OFF-en
Where is the viewpoint?	Wo ist der Aussichtspunkt?	Wo isch dr Usichtspunkt?	Vo ist der OW-seecht-PUNKHT
How long is the hike?	Wie lange dauert die Wanderung?	Wie lang dauert d'Wanderig?	Vee LANG DOW-ert dee VAN-der-oong

F. Emergencies & Essentials

English	German	Swiss German	Pronunciation
Help!	Hilfe!	Hilf!	HIL-feh / HILF
I need a doctor	Ich brauche einen Arzt	Ich bruuche en Dokter	Ish BROW-che eye-nen ARTST
Call the police	Rufen Sie die Polizei	Rufed d'Polizei	ROO-fen zee POL-ee-tsai
Pharmacy	Apotheke	Apothek	AH-po-teh-keh
Emergency number	Notruf	Notruf	NOTE-roof
Lost & found	Fundbüro	Fundbüro	FOOND-bue-ro

How to Use This Cheat Sheet

- Keep this page bookmarked or printed while traveling.
- Use High German for menus, signs, and official settings.
- Use Swiss German words for greetings and casual conversations—it earns you instant warmth from locals.

CHAPTER 19: QUICK REFERENCE & RESOURCES

Read this first. Move faster when key numbers, apps, and contacts are in one place. Save this page to your phone.

Lift Schedules and Contacts

Jungfrau Railways (network status, reservations, help)

- Rail Info Interlaken, Höheweg 35, 3800 Interlaken.
- Tel: +41 33 828 72 33 | Email: info@jungfrau.ch
- Get live operating info and reservation requirements online.

Harder Kulm Funicular (Harderbahn)

- Valley Station: Talstation Harderbahn, 3800 Interlaken.
- Tel: +41 33 828 73 39
- Travel dates: April 18 – October 26, 2025. Depart every 30 minutes.

Schynige Platte Railway (SPB)

- Valley Station: Wilderswil.
- Season: June 21 – October 26, 2025. Travel time: about 52 minutes.

Grindelwald–First Gondola (Firstbahn)

- Valley station at Talstation Firstbahn, 3818 Grindelwald.
- Tel: +41 33 828 77 11.

Schilthorn–Piz Gloria Cableway

- Find Schilthorn Cableway Ltd at Lengwald 301, 3824 Stechelberg.
- Tel: +41 33 826 00 07 | Email: info@schilthorn.ch

Niederhornbahn

- Niederhornbahn AG, Schmockenstrasse 253, 3803 Beatenberg.
- Tel: +41 33 841 08 41 | Email: info@niederhorn.ch

Key information and tips to make payments, manage Swiss Francs (CHF), and ensure smooth transactions while traveling. Avoid surprises with this guidance.

- Pay in CHF on card terminals to avoid conversion fees.
- Use contactless payments widely; keep cash for kiosks and mountain huts.
- Locate ATMs at Interlaken Ost and West stations.
- Always carry a backup card with an active PIN.

Contact details and immediate action steps for emergencies, as well as essential safety and security information for both travelers and locals.

- Interlaken Tourism, Marktgasse 1, 3800 Interlaken.
- Tel: +41 33 826 53 00 | Coordinates: 46.685070, 7.853850

Transport Assistance

- SBB Contact Center: 0848 44 66 88 (24/7).
- BLS Travel Centre Interlaken West: Bahnhofstrasse 28, 3800 Interlaken | Tel: +41 58 327 47 50.

Weather and Alerts

- **Use MeteoSwiss App** for forecasts and rain radar.
- **Use AlertSwiss App** for civil protection alerts and safety guidance.

Immediate access to local hospitals and pharmacies, with locations and contacts for medical help when you need it most.

- **Amavita Interlaken**, Höheweg 59 | Tel: +41 33 822 48 54
- **Apotheke Dr. Portmann AG**, Höheweg 4 | Tel: +41 33 822 17 23

Official Links and Apps

Transport

- Use SBB Mobile for train schedules, ticket purchases, and live platforms.
- Use the Jungfrau Railways App for lift status updates, reservations, and seasonal information.

Safety and Weather

- Check MeteoSwiss for weather forecasts, warnings, and radar maps.
- Check AlertSwiss for real-time civil alerts and emergency updates.
- Rega App – Direct GPS-enabled rescue assistance.

Trails and Maps

- Use SwitzerlandMobility for official hiking, biking, and sledging routes, with offline downloads available.

Other Helpful Tools

- Check the SwissTopo Map Viewer for detailed contour maps.
- Use an offline German/Swiss German translator for communication.
- Set currency converters to the CHF base.
- Carry a portable power bank for day-long hiking trips.

Apps and Offline Setup

- Sign in to SBB Mobile, add payment details, and save tickets for offline checks.
- Add Interlaken, Jungfraujoch, and Schilthorn to MeteoSwiss favorites.

- Enable location-based push notifications in AlertSwiss.
- Download SwitzerlandMobility maps offline before leaving Wi-Fi coverage.

Troubleshooting FAQ

Missed Train

- Regular tickets: board the next available train within the allowed window.
- Rebook Supersaver or reserved-seat tickets via app or counter.

Sudden Storm

- Leave ridges/open spaces immediately.
- Seek shelter in stations, gondola stations, or restaurants during storms.
- Check MeteoSwiss for live radar updates and weather warnings.

Lost Pass or Ticket

- Block and replace SwissPass travel cards via the SBB Contact Center.
- Retrieve e-tickets via your account; a valid ID is required for verification.

Closed Lift

- Check Jungfrau Railways for live operating updates on lifts.
- If closed: Harder Kulm → Niederhorn; Schynige Platte → Männlichen/First.

Fast Contacts Index

- Rail Info Interlaken: +41 33 828 72 33
- SBB Contact Center: 0848 44 66 88

- Interlaken Tourism: +41 33 826 53 00
- Spital Interlaken Emergency: +41 33 826 26 26
- Schilthorn Cableway: +41 33 826 00 07
- Niederhornbahn: +41 33 841 08 41

Appendix: Packing Lists by Season

Packing for Interlaken requires striking a balance between comfort, practicality, and preparedness. Weather in the Bernese Oberland can shift quickly, especially at higher altitudes. The right gear ensures you stay warm, dry, and ready for unexpected changes.

A.1 Spring and Autumn Essentials *(March–May | September–November)*

Spring and autumn in Interlaken bring mild daytime temperatures but cool mornings and evenings. Rain showers are frequent, so layering and waterproofing are essential.

Clothing & Layers

- Lightweight waterproof shell jacket (GORE-TEX or similar)
- Insulating mid-layer fleece or light down jacket
- Long-sleeve thermal tops for cooler days
- Breathable hiking shirts (synthetic or merino wool)
- Convertible hiking pants for flexibility

Footwear & Accessories

- Waterproof hiking boots with good ankle support
- Merino wool socks to manage moisture
- Lightweight gloves and a beanie for chilly mornings
- Compact, packable umbrella or rain poncho

Pro Tips

- Always pack a light insulating layer, even on sunny days — alpine winds are unpredictable.
- Carry a dry bag for electronics when hiking to protect them from moisture.

A.2 Summer Daypacks and Rain Plans *(June–August)*

Summer in Interlaken is warm and lively, but sudden alpine storms are common, especially in July and August. Pack light, breathable clothing, but prepare for unexpected weather changes.

Clothing & Layers

- Quick-dry hiking shirts and shorts
- Lightweight UV-protection layer or long-sleeve sun shirt
- Packable rain jacket or poncho for sudden showers
- Swimsuit for lakes, lidos, or river rafting

Daypack Must-Haves

- 20–30L hiking backpack with hydration system
- Hat or cap with sun protection
- Sunglasses with UV400 protection
- Travel-sized sunscreen (SPF 30+)
- Reusable water bottle (Interlaken has free public fountains)

Pro Tips

- The weather can swing from 30°C sunny valleys to 10°C at Jungfraujoch — always bring a warm layer.
- Store snacks and a microfiber towel for unplanned lake dips.

A.3 Winter Layers, Traction, and Cold-Weather Gear *(December–February)*

Interlaken winters are magical, with nearby ski resorts and snowshoeing trails. Average daytime temperatures range from **5°C to +5°C**, requiring proper insulation and weatherproofing.

Clothing & Layers

- **Base layer:** Thermal merino top and bottoms
- **Mid-layer:** Insulated fleece or down jacket
- **Outer shell:** Waterproof, windproof ski jacket and pants
- Insulated gloves, neck gaiter, and wool beanie
- Warm socks (avoid cotton; choose merino or synthetic blends)

Footwear & Snow Gear

- Waterproof winter boots with solid traction
- Microspikes or snow grips for icy trails
- Ski goggles or sunglasses for glare protection

Pro Tips

- Utilize layering techniques, including base, insulation, and shell, for optimal temperature control.
- Carry hand warmers for longer ski or sledging days.

A.4 Waterproofing, Footwear, and Accessories *(All Seasons)*

Regardless of when you visit, Interlaken's alpine climate demands a year-round essentials kit:

Waterproofing Gear

- High-quality rain jacket and rain pants
- Waterproof backpack cover for hikes

- Dry bags for electronics and documents

Footwear Checklist

- Hiking boots with Vibram soles for summer/autumn
- Winter boots with insulation and grip
- Comfortable city shoes for casual walks

Essential Accessories

- Compact power bank for phones and cameras
- Lightweight trekking poles for steeper hikes
- Collapsible shopping bag (eco-friendly and practical)
- Small first-aid kit for blisters and minor injuries

Pro Tips

- Always check the MeteoSwiss app before heading out.
- Store extra socks, gloves, and layers in a waterproof pouch.

MAPS

Interlaken Airport

Interlaken Hotels

BONUS SECTION

Interlaken Trivia Quiz & Puzzles

Whether you're planning your first visit or reliving your Interlaken memories, this trivia and puzzle section adds a little fun to your travel experience. Test your knowledge, solve challenges, and discover quirky facts about this alpine paradise.

Questions

1. Which two lakes surround Interlaken?
   A) Lake Geneva & Lake Lucerne
   B) Lake Thun & Lake Brienz
   C) Lake Zurich & Lake Zug
   D) Lake Neuchâtel & Lake Biel
2. What is the name of the famous mountain peak offering panoramic views of Interlaken?
   A) Schynige Platte
   B) Jungfraujoch
   C) Harder Kulm
   D) Männlichen
3. Interlaken is known as the gateway to which UNESCO World Heritage site?
   A) Swiss Alps Jungfrau-Aletsch
   B) Lavaux Vineyards
   C) Bern Old Town
   D) Rhine Falls
4. Which activity is Interlaken considered the European capital of?
   A) Paragliding
   B) Kayaking
   C) Rock Climbing
   D) Hot Air Ballooning
5. Where can you take the famous "Top of Europe" train ride?
   A) Harder Kulm
   B) Jungfraujoch
   C) Schilthorn
   D) First Grindelwald

6. What is the name of the charming village near Interlaken known for its stunning waterfalls?
   A) Lauterbrunnen
   B) Grindelwald
   C) Wengen
   D) Mürren
7. Which local railway offers one of the steepest cogwheel journeys in the world?
   A) Pilatusbahn
   B) Harderbahn
   C) Schynige Platte Railway
   D) Jungfrau Railway
8. Which of these activities is most popular on Lake Thun?
   A) Whale Watching
   B) Sunset Cruises
   C) Surfing
   D) Cliff Diving
9. What is Interlaken's traditional greeting in Swiss German?
   A) Grüezi
   B) Hallo
   C) Bonjour
   D) Servus
10. Where can you find the famous revolving restaurant featured in the James Bond movie *On Her Majesty's Secret Service*?
    A) Jungfraujoch
    B) Schilthorn (Piz Gloria)
    C) Harder Kulm
    D) Niesen
11. What is the approximate elevation of Harder Kulm?
    A) 800 m
    B) 1,322 m
    C) 1,850 m
    D) 2,200 m
12. Which Interlaken Museum showcases local culture and history?
    A) Jungfrau Museum
    B) Ballenberg Museum
    C) Swiss Alpine Museum
    D) Tourist Museum Interlaken

13. Which extreme sport involves descending into gorges and waterfalls using ropes and slides?
    A) Rafting
    B) Canyoning
    C) Abseiling
    D) Ziplining
14. What is the name of Interlaken's central park, popular for picnics and festivals?
    A) Höhematte Park
    B) Lindenhof Park
    C) Rosengarten
    D) Wengen Gardens
15. What currency is used in Interlaken?
    A) Euro (€)
    B) Swiss Franc (CHF)
    C) US Dollar ($)
    D) Pound Sterling (£)
16. Which mountain station offers spectacular hiking routes and alpine gardens?
    A) Schynige Platte
    B) Jungfraujoch
    C) Kleine Scheidegg
    D) Grindelwald First
17. Where can visitors enjoy night sledging in winter near Interlaken?
    A) Mürren
    B) Axalp
    C) Niederhorn
    D) Beatenberg
18. Which lake is known for its turquoise-blue waters and kayaking tours?
    A) Lake Lucerne
    B) Lake Thun
    C) Lake Brienz
    D) Lake Maggiore
19. What is Interlaken most famous for globally?
    A) Chocolate Festivals
    B) Adventure Sports
    C) Ski Resorts
    D) Shopping Malls

20. Which nearby peak offers a panoramic view of the Eiger, Mönch, and Jungfrau?
    A) Harder Kulm
    B) Schilthorn
    C) Niesen
    D) First Grindelwald

Answer Key

1. B) Lake Thun & Lake Brienz
2. C) Harder Kulm
3. A) Swiss Alps Jungfrau-Aletsch
4. A) Paragliding
5. B) Jungfraujoch
6. A) Lauterbrunnen
7. D) Jungfrau Railway
8. B) Sunset Cruises
9. A) Grüezi
10. B) Schilthorn (Piz Gloria)
11. B) 1,322 m
12. D) Tourist Museum Interlaken
13. B) Canyoning
14. A) Höhematte Park
15. B) Swiss Franc (CHF)
16. A) Schynige Platte
17. D) Beatenberg
18. C) Lake Brienz
19. B) Adventure Sports
20. A) Harder Kulm

INTERLAKEN

N	J	U	N	G	F	R	A	U	E	T	T
T	H	U	N	R	E	R	K	U	L	M	G
B	R	I	E	N	Z	T	H	U	N	V	C
A	R	A	G	L	I	D	I	N	G	A	A
A	P	L	S	C	H	Y	N	I	G	G	A
A	L	P	S	B	E	A	T	U	S	I	S
I	G	R	E	E	Z	I	A	L	P	S	N
I	S	E	N	F	L	U	H	I	E	N	L
S	E	E	L	I	S	B	E	R	G	L	U
G	R	U	E	Z	I	A	L	P	S	E	E
B	E	A	T	U	S	I	S	E	N	F	L	U	H

INTERLAKEN   JUNGFRAU
HARDERKULM   LAUTERBRUNNEN
BRIENZ   THUNN
PARAGLIDING   CANYONING
CANYONING   LUCERNE
SCHYNIGE   ALPS
LUCERNE   ISENFLUH

Interlaken Travel Journal & Planner

Traveler's Details

Name:		Contact:	
Trip Dates:			

Daily Planner

Date:		Day:		Weather:		Temperature:	
Morning Plans		Afternoon Adventures		Evening Highlights			

Must-Visit Spots Checklist

■ Jungfraujoch	■ Harder Kulm	■ Lauterbrunnen
■ Schynige Platte	■ Lake Brienz	■ Lake Thun
■ Grindelwald	■ Schilthorn	■ Höhematte Park

Expense Tracker (CHF)

Date	Location	Activity	Cost (CHF)

Memorable Moments

Use this space to jot down highlights, unforgettable experiences, or personal reflections during your Interlaken journey.

Photo Log

Attach printed photos here or note memorable photo spots and captions.

Packing Notes

■ Hiking Boots	■ Waterproof Jacket	■ Travel Passes
■ Photography Gear	■ Sunglasses & Sunscreen	■ Power Bank

Interlaken Travel Journal & Planner

Traveler's Details

Name:		Contact:	
Trip Dates:			

Daily Planner

Date:		Day:		Weather:		Temperature:	
Morning Plans		Afternoon Adventures		Evening Highlights			

Must-Visit Spots Checklist

■ Jungfraujoch	■ Harder Kulm	■ Lauterbrunnen
■ Schynige Platte	■ Lake Brienz	■ Lake Thun
■ Grindelwald	■ Schilthorn	■ Höhematte Park

Expense Tracker (CHF)

Date	Location	Activity	Cost (CHF)
_____	_____	_____	_____
_____	_____	_____	_____

Memorable Moments

Use this space to jot down highlights, unforgettable experiences, or personal reflections during your Interlaken journey.

Photo Log

Attach printed photos here or note memorable photo spots and captions.

Packing Notes

■ Hiking Boots	■ Waterproof Jacket	■ Travel Passes
■ Photography Gear	■ Sunglasses & Sunscreen	■ Power Bank

Printed in Dunstable, United Kingdom